THE MIND GAME OF MMA

THE MIND GAME OF MMA

12 Lessons To Develop The Mental Toughness
Essential To Becoming A Champion

By Kevin Seaman

Published by Center Line Press
326 Barrington Rd.
Syracuse, NY 13045

Printed in the United States of America.
ISBN: 978-0-9839214-3-1
Center Line Press
326 Barrington Rd.
Syracuse, NY 13045

Cover Graphic: ©istockphoto.com, Cover Design: Kevin Seaman
Foreword By Phil Migliarese III

Visit us at thewinningmindset.com / or ewmaa.com

TABLE OF CONTENTS

Acknowledgements

This is a book I've had in my mind for a long while, it was inspired by the phenomenal coaches and teachers I have had the great privilege and opportunity to train with through my 40 years in the martial arts and my 57 years of living.

To my first and best coaches, my Mom and Dad, thank you for the direction you continued to try to point me in. Congratulations, it worked.

To Guro Dan Inosanto, thank you for all you have taught me, and giving me the inspiration necessary to "Always be a White Belt at something."

To Ajarn Chai Sirisute, thank you for showing me I could always "Be More than I am" and helping me to do so.

To Sifu Francis Fong, thank you for all your emotional inspiration, the priceless training in martial arts, and your friendship through the years. You are a truly unique individual.

To Donna, thank you for encouraging me to write this, and standing by me. You are my girl, you are my best friend, and the love I've found with you is something most people just dream of.

To my coaches in personal development and mental performance, Jim Brault, Brian Tracy, Anthony Robbins, and the countless others that have influenced me as a coach, thank you for your guidance and your knowledge.

To Phil Migliarese, thank you for taking the time and energy to write the foreword for my book. Your influence on so many, your skill as a teacher and technician, and your diligence to become a strong leader has made you truly wise beyond our years. Thanks for being who you are.

To my students, and those I've had the opportunity to coach, help reach your goals and exceed your potential, thank you for allowing me that opportunity.

To you, the reader, thank you for your interest in making yourself that much better. Without you, I would have little encouragement to write and share the priceless lessons in this book.

"Winners dwell on and hold the self-image of that person they would most like to become. They get a vivid, clear, emotional, sensory picture of themselves as if they had already achieved that new role in their life."

This book is dedicated to the men and women who have or seek that vision.

About The Author

Kevin Seaman began his formal martial arts training in 1970. To date he has achieved advanced instructor levels in seven different martial arts systems, totaling eight black belts, is a certified boxing coach, Thai Boxing Association USA Full Instructor Level under Ajarn Chai Sirisute, certified police defensive tactics instructor, published author, and certified personal trainer. He also has an extensive background in exercise physiology, strength and conditioning, mental performance, and nutrition.

Bruce Lee's Top Student and Protégé Mr. Daniel Inosanto personally trained him for over 28 years, Kevin having achieved one of the highest ranks awarded by Mr. Inosanto. His first book Jun Fan Gung Fu: Seeking The Path Of Jeet Kune Do was very well received internationally. Kevin owned and operated the East West Martial Arts Academy in Central New York for 19 years.

Kevin also maintains an impressive association of instructors and approximately 500 students throughout the USA. He offers his teaching skills through seminars, personal training and consultation and at a few select schools. He has also worked on the Instructional Staff in the Physical Education Department at Cornell University since 1992. Kevin is Internationally recognized as a teacher in the various martial arts he's studied and has taught over 10,000 students to date.

Kevin is a three time Hall of Fame inductee, being

inducted into the ZDK, AMA and World Martial Arts Hall of Fame, honored for a Diamond Lifetime Achievement Award in Atlantic City in 2001. At the age of 37 was a World Champion competing on the USA team in full contact stick fighting in south east Asia at the 1992 World, Kali, Arnis Championships at the Aquino Memorial Stadium in Manila, Philippines and a three time Eastern National Champion in full contact fighting.

Kevin has long been known for his ability in coaching individuals, both in and out of the competitive arena. He has been highly recognized for his book called The Winning Mind Set with co-author Jim Brault. The book is based on the system of personal achievement taught in his Sports Psychology course at Cornell University. Recently published, the book and Audio Book is an extraordinarily comprehensive, results oriented system of performance enhancement that has been used successfully by hundreds of individuals to date.

Foreword

Every winner needs a motivating Jedi master in their corner. If you are not lucky enough to have such a person in your corner, you should at least absorb his lessons. Lucky you! You happen to be holding a Jedi master's "how to" manual to mastering the mental game of MMA

I have known the author Kevin Seaman for over 20 years. I met him as a 12-year-old kid in Philadelphia, at beginning my journey in Gracie Brazilian Jiu-Jitsu and Muay Thai kickboxing. Kevin, a New York resident, would drive five hours to train with the master instructors that would visit our school in Philly. His dedication to learning from the source is one of the reasons why Kevin has earned 8 black belt levels in various martial arts and is one of the most sought after striking coaches for MMA.

Kevin is without a doubt a badass martial artist, but I find Kevin's personality to be his most interesting and inspiring dimension. He is always so positive and willing to absorb new information. Now after reading this book I realized how Kevin stays so "Zen". It is by his ability to "always frame things in a Positive, Personal and Present tense." This concept is powerful and occasionally a struggle for some of us, especially for those of us that are fighters, training for a competition. Mastery of this concept is vital to the fighter that is building momentum to MMA success.

Now, here it is twenty years later, I am a 4th degree black belt under Relson Gracie, a multiple school owner, coach to MMA fighters, and the head of one of the biggest teams in the world.

Kevin's book could not have been more on time to help me in the pursuit of excellence for the people that look to me for support. His book has helped me as a practitioner and as an MMA coach.

During my competitive days, one of the most important things to me was improving my "inner game". As a practitioner of yoga, I knew the importance of maintaining the mind. I always thought that I was a little different from most of the other Brazilian Jiu-Jitsu competitors. While the other guys were jumping around and running up and down the arena, I was on the warm up mat, composing my mind with breathing and yoga poses. The ultimate goal in yoga is to "know thy self". After years of practicing yoga, I found what got me mentally prepped for competition, and it was the "calming" and "psyching down" process. I would not have known that, had I not taken the time to do mental training necessary. Some fighters need to get "psyched up" before a fight. I didn't. I actually tried it once based off of a coach's vehement recommendation. I went out to my match and got exhausted in less than a minute. I felt that I was burnt out from the warm up and "psych up" before the match. I luckily pulled through the match successfully only because of my physical conditioning and endurance. In my next match, I went right back to calming myself before my match, and continued on to win the gold.

As an MMA coach, I find it difficult convincing the average MMA fighter of the importance of building the "mental game". It seems that fighters are more interested in the body. But when the playing field is level, and the other guy is just as fit, it is the fighter that is mentally toughest that will be the winner.

Here is my new plan to get through to those fighters: I am going to throw Kevin's new book into their hands and them tell them that UFC champion Jon Jones trains his "inner game" and called Kevin's last book, The Winning Mind Set, "Simply Brilliant!" Read it!

Kevin's step-by-step guidance is incredibly helpful. His forty years of martial arts experience has been compressed into twelve easy to understand lessons. In a matter of weeks you can develop new mental strategies to help overcome one of the most devastation opponents: Self-defeating thoughts.

If you are an MMA fighter, Kevin is the guy that you want in your corner. We have cornered UFC fighters together and I have seen first hand how valuable his coaching is. Not only will you have one the best Thai Boxing coaches in your corner, but a wise Jedi master as well.

Phil Migliarese III
- 4th degree black belt under Master Relson Gracie
- Owner of Balance Studios MMA
  Author of *Yoga For Fighters*
  BalanceStudios.net

Lesson One
Seeking Your Path

"It's amazing, in the BLINK of an eye you finally see the light." -Aerosmith

It's hard to describe, this burning desire. You think about it more each day, it's as if something from inside of you is pushing, driving you to do something that most people would never consider. You struggle to understand it, to make sense of this feeling, the excitement building within you to FIGHT. To some people who watch Mixed Martial Arts, it could be construed as unrestrained violence. To that untrained eye it is a chaotic flurry of human free for all. To you, however it is as technical as chess, more challenging then anything you've ever experienced. To you it is a quest, a quest for excellence that starts from within.
That is where we will begin, within...

It would be no surprise to anyone if I were to say that in Martial Athletics, also referred to as Combat Sports, you must be in exceptional condition to compete at a professional level. You know that it requires strength, cardio and muscular endurance, speed, incredible reflexes, flexibility and power. To compete in the big show, you must be technically, at a high level, you need to have a ferocious striking game and a phenomenal ground game. **But there's another game that's absolutely crucial to your success in this arena and that is "The Mind Game."**
As a professional martial artist and mental performance coach

I have had the amazing opportunity to meet and train with some amazing athletes and coaches. One of the qualities that these individuals had that set them apart from everyone else is this; they've discovered **the secrets to unleashing the power of their mind.**

In this book I will share with you the **secrets** that they used to separate themselves from their competition, into a class above everyone else as competitors, coaches, martial artists and people. Not only have I applied these strategies to hundreds of success driven competitors but, I have used them to personally fight full contact in South East Asia and become a world champion at nearly 40 years old, achieve the rank of eight separate Black Belts in various martial arts, and become a three-time Hall of Fame inductee, and one of the happiest, most energetic people I know. These "principle based" strategies took me over 20 years to compile. For the past decade I have taught aspects of this success system to dozens of students, coaches and athletes on an exclusively private basis, and semi-private workshops, and now in this book I am going to teach it to you!

I've compiled the book into easy to read, engaging Lessons, each one rich with valuable content to help you develop your mind in the direction of your personal path to success.

As a coach, the single most important thing to me is, and always will be RESULTS! It's not what or how much you know; it's how and when you use it that will determine your results. In other words, it's not what you know. It's what you **do,** that makes you successful. So, read on and let's see how that applies to MMA.

A fighter can train in multiple disciplines with various top coaches, instructors and trainers. He can study with the best, learning hundreds of locks, be able to transition smoothly when defending or attacking from every position, he can learn some of the most effective Tricks Of The Trade that Muay Thai and other Combat Sports training with a top coach can offer, yet he will only use a few technical aspects to win. In order to determine what to do, at that moment that will bring him a successful outcome, he must also be totally committed to doing everything possible to train his sub-conscious in all aspects of the sport.

Throughout the book you may see some of the same messages or principles applied in different contexts. Key Principles are just THAT, KEYS that will unlock your potential, therefore these laws of success will be used in various examples. Many of these will be used conjunctively and with strategies for their application. I've compiled a list of some of these Key Principles at the end of the book.

I want to impress upon you from the beginning that if you want the success you're capable of, you must be disciplined and do the WORK, not just read the book passively. I have included several journal pages in the back of the book for you to write in. I encourage you to also get a notebook to record the things you learn on the mat, in the school and in your fight training. This alone may be **the most valuable thing you will ever do** to accelerate your progress. So, let's start on your path to make you the best Fighter or Competitor you can be.

"Do the things today that others will not do, so you can live a life tomorrow that others will not live."- Kevin Seaman

Lesson Two
Building Your Mental Toolbox

"Our Mind always leads us in the direction of our dominant thoughts." -Kevin Seaman

A Question Of Balance

I ask every athlete and coach these two questions, and I am now going to ask you. First, "In competition, how much of an athlete's success is attributed to their physical ability and how much is based on the mental aspects that an individual possesses and utilizes?" My question has been confirmed with a variety of statements, 50/50, 30% physical and 70% mental are the usual, yet all will admit that the mental component is critical to a the outcome. I have trained amateur and high-level Pro fighters for decades and I know the kind of ass-busting physical commitment that is required during a training camp to get in "fighting shape". If you have a great coach you work both offense and defense. You work hard to be in peak condition, you work your standup, your footwork, your takedowns, your clinch, and you work your grappling game.

Now here's my second question. "So, what do you do to train your Mind Game?" At this point most people just stare off searching for an answer. I have the answer! First of all, winning is a state of mind. If you aren't training the mental aspects needed to be the best in competition, you're at most training at 50% of your potential.

As a teacher and coach of martial arts and martial athletics for over 35 years it is obvious to me that prior to, and during competition the mental aspects that are used by the performer are absolutely as crucial as are the physical qualities. It is what we call a critical success factor, which we will cover in complete detail later.

A Mental Toolbox

In this book, I will give you some valuable keys utilized by many of the top athletes in the world and formulated by some of the leading coaches. Let's start by building a Mental Toolbox, filled with the basic tools necessary to become the fighter or coach that you want to be. Here are the first five tools. As we progress through each lesson, we will add to your Mental Toolbox.

#1 A Belief in Yourself and Your Team- Your beliefs are based on the references you focus on, which in turn support that belief. These references (experiences) can be first hand (personal), second hand (you were told, you read, you saw), or imagined references and can substantiate your empowerment, giving you confidence or also create the opposite effect, depending on your mindset. Our mind works by moving us in the direction of what we focus on. Focusing on our losses (what we don't want) supports the belief that we will lose again and directs us toward all the possibilities surrounding our losses. In contrast, when we focus on our wins, we create a sense of strength through the possibility of continued victory. **Our mind always leads us in the direction of our dominant thoughts.**

"If you believe, then you have already taken the first step towards your achievement."-Rickson Gracie

#2 Visualize To Win- See it, then achieve it. Athletes have long used mental imagery prior to an event, just as warriors have before engaging in battle. Did you know that your subconscious mind can't really tell the difference between experiencing something vividly in your mind and actually doing it? In fact, the neuro-receptors in your brain respond almost identically. Your thoughts, self-talk and inner visions (visualizations) are electrochemical events that affect your performance on every level. Visualizing is a skill that needs to be honed, just like footwork, throws, positioning, locking and striking. When visualizing, focus on these four keys-Vividness, Frequency, Consistency, and Duration. When using the four qualities for visual success of vividness, frequency, consistency, and duration, you will see amazing results in your overall performance. This may just be the missing key that will unlock your potential and take you to a level you've never before achieved. When you see yourself performing with intensity and emotion over and over, focused on the outcome you expect, your subconscious accepts that as real. Your BELIEFS, become your REALITY. It will be convincingly apparent by your outward confidence that you are completely committed toward your directive, and you will perform as though it were another victory. See it first in your mind's eye and then achieve it in your LIFE.

#3 There Are Voices In My Head- Did you know that research has found that we talk to ourselves nearly 50,000 times a day, everyday? That's nearly 375,000 times a week, 1,500,000 times a month, and 19,500,000 a year. In fact, you're talking to yourself right now. You're probably saying something like, "That's amazing! I didn't know that " or "How's that possible?" Just as you talk to yourself, so does everyone and this "self talk" is many times what directs you in your actions. Sometimes these inner dialogs aren't dialogs at all, they are in the form of emotions, pictures, scenes and thought messages. And, despite all the media stimulus shouting out at us constantly, conversations with our coaches, friends, family, co-workers, and acquaintances, etc... Guess WHO we listen to the most attentively? Ourselves! Not only that but, most of what the majority of people say to themselves is negative in context. "This sucks, why's this always gotta happen to me? God, I hope I don't get injured before the fight. What's this knucklehead's problem? Why can't I just once get a break?" Sound familiar? This internal dialog goes on both on a cognitive level, as well as subconsciously. So, pay particular attention to your internal voice. Always state things in the Positive, Personal and Present tense. Tell yourself exactly what you want...never what you don't want! *Example:* I don't want to blow this fight. *Better Example:* I always do the very best I can. I got this one in the bag. I'm in the best shape. I've beat this guy! Remember our FIRST Tool in this section?

"When you start by doing what's necessary, then you begin doing what's possible, then before you know it you're doing what most people consider the impossible!" - Kevin Seaman

#4 Never, Never, Ever Give Up- There is a defined procedure to developing what we know as Mental Toughness. Here are four of many, of the mental qualities necessary to be the fighter you want to be. Each of the four qualities will support each other, strengthening your behavior and mindset synergistically.

Emotional Flexibility- Going with what comes. This quality is the ability to make the very best out of every experience and outcome. Being flexible is remaining balanced and resourceful, accepting responsibility for your outcome, rather than being defensive, blaming and rigid. These latter behaviors are a sign of weakness, and are the result of fear-based emotions. Much of this pertains to how you process the experience, your internal dialog and your ability to manage your emotional state.

Emotional Strength- This is all about having a sound belief in yourself and what the outcome will be. To remain emotionally strong means doing so under extreme pressure, to continue to maintain your fighting spirit even under seemingly impossible odds. To harness your greatest strength when the emotional pressure is the utmost, and resist and exert to your full potential in spite of it. Emotional Strength is, in essence, expecting more out of yourself than anyone possibly could.

Emotional Responsiveness- This is the ability to remain engaged and connected with the moment and respond without hesitation. All habits are built through repetition. Your emotional responsiveness will be a product of your habits. Visualizing a successful outcome repeatedly in your mind substantiates your desired result and this familiarizes your subconscious with what you want to achieve over and over. Hesitation often comes from internal conflict in beliefs, emotions and personal values.

Emotional Resiliency- Resiliency is not giving up, bouncing back, staying on track, using that very moment when your actions didn't give you the results necessary to get the long-term results you desire. Resiliency is the ability **to tap into** your emotional power, not allowing it to **tap you out** of your objective. Remember, the key is to not just see your goals, but to feel the emotions connected to achieving your goals and never, never ever give up on your key goal.

#5 Take A Personal Inventory- What exactly makes a person perform better? It's hard to pinpoint exactly why one person excels far beyond his or her competitive peers. What winning combination do these "Top Achievers" possess that sets them apart? Why is the margin sometimes so pronounced? Why did Michael Jordan standout? What allowed Gretzsky to dominate on the ice? Why is the name Rickson associated with greatness? What were the qualities that made Ali the seemingly unstoppable champ?

Let's not stop at sports, there must be one distinct feature that sets the top achievers in every field in a category of excellence that is exponentially unique! I've heard some say, it's genetics. But, is it?

Over 40 years ago, the world famous Martial Arts Master, Bruce Lee studied this same query. Lee was totally obsessed with the question of what made the superior athlete, technician, or warrior. I began reading about Bruce Lee and studying with his protégé Dan Inosanto, over 25 years ago. This is where I first learned about Mixed Martial Arts (Lee was one of the pioneers) and the concept of how to concentrate on improving the defining *"Qualities or Attributes"* that made someone a top achiever or champion. Really, it is these attributes that create the combination that is superior.

So, what are attributes? Attributes are strengths that attribute to or help make up who you are, sort of like personal assets. In order for us to have a clear distinction of our capability, aptitude and our potential, we need to consider what our areas of strengths and weaknesses may be. So far, I have identified some of our necessary skills in the areas of mental imagery and internal communication. We have also confirmed that our beliefs are in part relevant to our own perception of our strengths and deficiencies. These are some of the elements that contribute to the make up of our identity, of who we are. But, it goes much deeper than that. Our attributes can be both psychological and physical in nature and can be naturally adopted skills and traits, or specifically learned and cultivated. I believe that all attributes can be improved to some degree. It also appears that there are certain attributes that are absolutely crucial, if not critical, for any marked success in given field. When we have that critical combination of attributes, necessary to succeed in our chosen endeavor developed to a level outstanding to that of our competition, we increase our chances for success beyond what we would have ever believed possible! A study at Harvard University concluded that in every career endeavor there is a set of 5-6 specific skill sets known as Critical Success Factors (CSF), that are crucial to the high level success of that challenge. It goes on to say that if one of these CSF's is inefficient, it will bring down the level of the remaining factors. These Critical Success Factors are important to recognize in yourself and others, and may hold the key to your personal development potential and a better understanding of your opponent.

"In life you perform things in a manner which develops the body asymmetrically, so in training you must develop the body symmetrically."
- Bob Gambitta

So let's take inventory. First you must identify what qualities the most outstanding people in your chosen field possess that make them outstanding.

Now, on the next page, write their names and next to their name list these qualities/attributes. Identify and write which of these qualities you believe are Critical Success Factors.

Outstanding Competitor Qualities That Make Them Stand Out

Now investigate your personal qualities and areas of necessary improvement introspectively with absolute honesty. Think about this and put together an inventory list of your best and worst qualities. The BEST way to improve to the level necessary to become the fighter/ athlete you want to be is to be brutally honest. If you have difficulty seeing a clear picture of your list, ask your coach or training partner for input. **You are on the way to making some of the most important distinctions for improving your future success and performance that you have ever made in your LIFE!** Now that you know what you possess, strengthen it. Now that you know what needs improvement, change it. The best way to improve something (or strengthen it) is to simply find the activities that most exemplify that skill and do them, as much as possible. Revise the level of intensity and difficulty when necessary as your specific skill evolves. This attribute specific cross training will do more to improve you than you would ever imagine. Don't believe me! Believe yourself and try it. Start NOW! Turn the page and READ the next chapter!

"When it's all said and done, there's a lot more said than done!"
-Lou Holtz-World Class Coach

Lesson Three
Building Blocks To Greatness

"What lies behind us and what lies before us are small matters compared to what lies within us." Ralph Waldo Emerson

Who are you? How do you see yourself? What qualities do you possess that make you unique, perhaps even an anomaly? Pretty simple questions aren't they? Or are they?

Most people don't stop to think just how important their identity is. Yet, it is your personal identity that is one of the most powerful influences on your behavior, directing you to your destination of success or devastation in a way most of us never realize. Do you think having the identity of a BJJ Black Belt will affect the way someone interacts on the mat? Do you think an identity as a member of a certain gang affects what a street kid will or will not do? Do you think identifying oneself as a winner changes the way someone approaches competition? How about seeing oneself as a coach, would that adjust the way one interacts with athletes? The answers are all undeniably YES!

For some, an identity may be congruent with their title or nickname. When you read names like Anderson "The Spider" Silva, Jon "Bones" Jones, Tito "The Huntington Beach Bad Boy" Ortiz, Randy "The Natural" Corture, BJ "The Prodigy" Penn or Chuck "The Iceman" Lidell. Don't they conjure up a strong, consistent image of how each fighter performs...and an identity?

How Do I Know Who I Am?
OK, let's take a look at exactly what comprises your identity. Your identity has three components. The first is your self-concept, how you perceive yourself. Simply put, your self-concept refers to those beliefs you have acquired that relate directly to you. This personal self-concept has a tremendous effect on the decisions you make

31

from moment to moment, determines the way you behave, and the way you perform at every activity. It determines whether you NEVER give up or make excuses for why you quit.

The second component is your self-image. Your self-image is the picture you have of yourself in your mind. It's the belief system you have adopted about yourself and the images they produce inside you. Your self-image is the KEY to human personality and behavior, and it is that undeniable self-image that sets the boundaries of individual accomplishment. It will define what you can and cannot be or do.

"Expand the self-image and you expand the area of the possible. The development of an adequate, realistic self-image will seem to imbue the individual with new capabilities, new talents and literally turn failure into success." -Maxwell Maltz

Your self-esteem is your third component to your unique identity; it is the emotional component of how you feel about yourself. More specifically, it is how you feel about the self-image your mind has created. It is not your physical image, it is your mental image, your inner mirror.

Why is it so important to understand the components of your identity? Because the more we understand ourselves and the depth of our character,

I.E. our identity, the better we are able to utilize our unique, personal strengths to guide us to success. If we are truly honest with ourselves, we will also realize our shortcomings and have more clarity about ways to improve our areas that are not strong.

"Knowledge in martial arts actually means self-knowledge. A martial artist has to take responsibility for himself and accept the consequences of his own doing."-Bruce Lee

We Are All Unique

Did you know that with your identity comes your code of conduct, and this set of rules governs your behavior? These rules can be well known, published or unwritten and understood. These rules can propel us to greatness, or can limit our potential dramatically. They can help us to achieve new heights, skyrocketing our success, or they can drag us down and prevent us from reaching what we desire. According to personal development expert Brian Tracy, each of us has a UHC or combination of Unique Human Capabilities. Your UHC is like a personal inventory, a statement of what you have and of what you need to do more of. It is your competitive advantage! Tracy goes on to say, your unique combination of human qualities, skills and behaviors are so unique that the odds are 50 billion to one that there is someone out there just like you!

Finding The Keys To Unlocking Your UHC

So, what exactly is it that makes a person perform better than their competition? It's hard to pinpoint exactly why one person excels far beyond their competitive peers. Why is the margin sometimes so pronounced? Why is Georges St. Pierre so hard to beat? Why is it so hard to land a glove on Anderson Silva? And when he is in peak condition, why is BJ Penn so obviously a prodigy? What winning combination do these "Top Achievers" possess that sets them apart? Let's not stop at MMA, or even at sports, there must be one distinct feature that sets the top achievers in every field in a category of excellence that is exponentially unique? I've heard people say it's simply genetics. But is it?

Remember what I said in the last chapter about Bruce Lee? How he studied the qualities that made a fighter the BEST? According to Bruce Lee's protégé, Dan Inosanto, Bruce worked daily to develop himself physically, psychologically, emotionally and spiritually. He studied and applied daily the *Qualities or Attributes* that made someone a top achiever or champion. Bruce was absolutely determined to create a system with a combination of physical and psychological qualities that was superior, in order for him to become the BEST.

"The fight is won or lost far away from witnesses - behind the lines, in the gym, and out there on the road, long before I dance under those lights." –Muhammad Ali

The First Key

What are attributes? Attributes are strengths that attribute to or help make up who you are, sort of like a list of personal assets. In order for us to have a clear distinction of our capability, aptitude and indeed our potential, we need to consider what our strengths and weaknesses may be. Our attributes can be both psychological and physical in nature and can be naturally adopted skills and traits, or specifically learned and cultivated. I believe that all attributes can be improved to some degree. It would also appear that certain attributes are absolutely crucial, if not critical, for any marked success in most every field. When you have that critical combination of attributes necessary to succeed in our chosen field developed to a level outstanding to that of your competition, you increase your chances for success beyond what you would have ever believed possible!

Think about this and review in your mind what attributes you possess, then list them in the Key Exercise on the page below.

Key Exercise # 1

List four of your personal psychological attributes, which you feel you are strong at, and four that you feel weak at or would like to improve. Examples: Focus, persistence, clarity, confidence, work ethic, assertiveness, etc…

Strong	Needs Improvement
1._____	1._____
2._____	2._____
3._____	3._____
4._____	4._____

Now list two different methods you could use for continued development or improvement of each of these psychological attributes. Work to improve each of these to the best of your ability.

1._____ 2._____
1._____ 2._____
1._____ 2._____
1._____ 2._____

1._____ 2._____
1._____ 2._____
1._____ 2._____
1._____ 2._____

Now list four of your personal physical attributes, which you feel you are strong at and four that you feel you are weak at or would like to improve. Examples: balance, flexibility, strength, speed, timing, coordination, etc…

Strong	**Needs Improvement**
1._____	1._____
2._____	2._____
3._____	3._____
4._____	4._____

Now list two different methods you could use for continued development or improvement of each of these physical attributes.

1._____ 2._____
1._____ 2._____
1._____ 2._____
1._____ 2._____

1._____ 2._____
1._____ 2._____
1._____ 2._____
1._____ 2._____

Work to improve each of these, as well, to the best of your ability.

Key Exercise # 2

Let's take this a step further. As I mentioned in the last Lesson, according to studies conducted at Harvard University, there are usually four or five Critical Success Factors (CSF's) In everything you do. These CSF's are things you must do in order to be successful in what you set out to accomplish. If you have a weakness in any one of your Critical Success Factors, it can bring all of your strong CSF's down dramatically. CSF's are more than just personal attributes, they are absolutely essential qualities or skills.

An example of an essential CSF in competitive MMA is cardiovascular endurance. You may be a great striker, have mad skills on the ground and shoot takedowns like a NCAA wrestler, but if your cardio is weak…you're done!

List below the Critical Success Factors necessary to succeed in MMA.

Take a moment to reflect on the critical success factors in MMA or any field you're challenged in. Identify them and rate yours from 1-5 as accurately and honestly as possible. **1-Poor, 2-Below Average, 3-Adequate, 4-Excellent, 5-Exceptional.**

You've identified these qualities in the top competitors in the sport. Now list them below.

Critical Success Factors In MMA

1) _____

2) _____

3) _____

4) _____

5) _____

"Fatigue makes cowards of us all."
- Vince Lombardi

36

How Can You Use This?

First you've identified what qualities the most outstanding people in MMA possess that make them outstanding. Then, you wrote these qualities/attributes in the columns provided. Next, you reflected and took a moment to investigate **your** personal qualities and areas of necessary improvement, and CSF's with brutal honesty. Where do you stand? What areas must you improve in? You are now on the way to making some of the most important distinctions for improving your future successes in the sport you love, that you have ever made in your LIFE!

How is this crucial to your performance? Do your homework and see for yourself. The more exceptional your personal CSF's, the greater your success will be in your GAME! These are the Building Blocks For Greatness that every great coach has kept as a secret weapon when developing great athletes!

"Slowness allows for sensitivity; sensitivity leads to structure; structure builds strength; strength is the essence of softness; softness is the prerequisite for speed; and speed (when predicated on all the attributes aforementioned) leads to supremacy."
 -Kenneth Jay

Lesson Four
Xerox® Your Best Performance

"Life is ten percent what happens to you and ninety percent how you respond to it." -Lou Holtz

What if you could duplicate your level of skill, emotion and intensity with carbon copy accuracy every time you practice and compete? What would it mean to you if you could accomplish this on a sub-conscious level by simply flipping a neurological switch in your head? Wouldn't this be useful, even valuable to you?

Some of the top athletes, peak performance experts, and high achievers use a specific technique to change their state of mind and emotionally jumpstart themselves from zero to full throttle instantly. I'm going to show you how!

Throughout these lessons I will use terms such as **"Visualize To Win"**-First you see it, then achieve it. For centuries athletes have long used mental imagery prior to an event, just as warriors have before engaging in battle. Because your subconscious mind can't really tell the difference between experiencing something vividly in your mind and actually doing it, you can use visualization to pre-experience events, better preparing you for that event. Science has proven that the neuro-receptors in your brain respond almost identically whether you are deeply visualizing or actually performing a task. Your thoughts, self-talk and inner visions (visualizations) are electrochemical events that affect your performance on every level. Visualizing is not easy to control. It's a mental skill that needs to be developed and honed, just like your physical skills in MMA, footwork, takedowns, positioning, locking and striking.

In this lesson, Lesson Four, I will teach you how to replicate the state of mind you had during your best performance using controlled visualization, while applying a technique and a series of exercises from Neuro-Linguistic Programming (NLP) known as Associative Anchoring. I've taught this exact method to hundreds, and it's in my second book, The Winning Mind Set.

What is Associative Anchoring?

Are you familiar with a man named Ivan Pavlov and his experiments with dogs? He was a scientist studying gastric secretions in dogs. In his study, he noticed something that intrigued him. The dogs were fed at specific intervals, accompanied by a ringing of a bell signaling that it was time to eat. He observed that when the dogs were about to be fed, they would salivate in anticipation of eating. He also learned that the dogs linked being fed to a ringing of the bell, and that they would salivate upon hearing the bell by itself, even without the sight or smell of the food. That bell, became an Anchor linked to eating, and caused the dogs to have a physiological reaction. The psychological action triggered a physiological response. If you have animals, you know that this phenomenon occurs with can openers, opening a cupboard door, or making a certain whistle. We are all influenced by associative *anchors* as well, and these *anchors* are links to associations we have experienced in our past. **Associations transport us back through time and space in an instant**

An _association_, then, is a learned or conditioned linkage between a mental and physical response and a stimulus (in this case the mental and physical response is anticipation of being fed, which produces excitement, a peak emotional state and salivation). An **_anchor_** is the stimulus that can **_trigger_** a certain response (the anchor here being the bell). The interesting thing is positive (or negative) associations become strongest when we are in a peak emotional state when influenced.

Step #1 Do a Personal Success History Search

Think back to a time when you performed at a peak level, when you were SHARP as a razor, so sharp, you amazed yourself. Visualize this event vividly with as much detail using your prime modalities (5 senses) and sub-modalities (distinctions of sensory details) to the greatest extent imaginable. If you see the venue, who's there? What colors do you see? Is it bright or dimly lit? Is it day or night? What color is your clothing or uniform? Are you seeing from behind your eyes (inside) or from outside your body, like a movie? Got it? Now do the same with the internal auditory and add that. What are you saying to yourself at that moment (internal auditory)? What sounds do you hear? What were others saying (external auditory)? Next use the same procedure for kinesthetic (feel), Gustatory (taste), and what olfactory (smells) you experienced. Finally, visualize using as much emotion as you can, stepping into your imagery. BE THERE! How do you feel? How are you standing, what are you thinking? What are you feeling emotionally? As you step into this event, visually pick about a two-minute mental film clip leading up to the climax. This is your personal Mental Film Clip. Keep playing the images in your head for as long as you can without losing focus. Some athletes use music to help them tune in for lengthy time spans, when using visual imagery, some use a quite environment. However you do it, stay with it as long as you can. Now, notice how you feel as you play the Mental Film Clip in your head. If you feel extremely excited, then you have associated this emotional state with your prior peak performance event. That's great!

Step#2 Find Your Anchor

Next find a combination of key words and movements that you may already do when you win, succeed or are happy. If you watch sports, you may notice that nearly every athlete has a ritual motion when they succeed. This ritual act you do is an Anchor you already have in place. Got it? If you don't have an anchor you can develop one that fits you and your level of intensity. Chuck Lidell used to run around the ring with his chin up, chest out and hands down after his win. Tito Ortiz jumped up and down bringing his knees up to his chest before he clashed with his opponent. Some people clinch one fist or through both hands in the air and yell. Keep your Anchor simple, quick powerful and unique, shout a key word as you do it. Yes! Kill it! Done!

Step #3 Setting Your Associative Anchor

Next combine your Mental Film Clip with your Anchor. To do this, play your Mental Film Clip through in your head with intensity and emotion. When you've come to the climax moment in your Mental Film Clip, fire your anchor! Now repeat the process 10-12 times until the Anchor sets. Play it over in your head with as much consistency and continuity as possible. Consistency is the key to success. Inconsistency creates just that, inconsistent results. Optimal results require some frequency. I recommend my clients practice their Anchor Setting Exercise a minimum of 3x a week in order to DRIVE it into their sub-conscious. Repetition is undoubtedly, the mother of skill. Research shows that when you repeat the same action (mentally or physically) a significant number of times, it becomes deeply ingrained in your subconscious and muscle memory.

Step#4 Test Your Anchor
Did your Anchor set? Let's test it and see. To test, simply fire your Anchor prior to your next training session. You should see and feel a marked difference in your performance, energy and intensity. If you feel a minor difference, then continue to drive the connection into your subconscious by repeating the exercise as needed.

"Winners have simply formed the habit of doing things losers don't like to do." -Albert Gray

What's The Bottom Line- When using the Associative Anchor strategy for success with vividness, frequency, consistency, and duration, you will see amazing results in your overall performance. This may just be the missing key that will unlock your potential and take you to a level, you've never achieved. I have several Anchors I use on a regular basis. One jacks me up, one calms me down, and one helps me focus more intensely. You can also use positive Anchors to collapse Anchors you may have to negative associations. To do this, visualize your negative association to a past event or performance and FIRE your positive Anchor several times as you focus on the negative association. You may want to have a fire extinguisher handy though.

"Keep away from people who try to be little your ambitions. Small people always do that, but the really great make you feel that you, to can become great."
-Mark Twain

Lesson Five
Reframing Your Possibilities

"Limitations live only in our minds. But if we use our imaginations, our possibilities become limitless."
- Jamie Paolinetti

Most of us have heard the term Frame Of Reference. The term actually comes from the way we perceive something due to our belief about that subject. In Lesson One, The Mental Toolbox, I briefly covered the implications our references play in what we believe to be true or false and how it pertains to MMA. References are supports that confirm why we feel something is actually the way we believe it is. OK, here's the punch line! **What you believe becomes your reality.** And, this is true regardless if it is actually, in reality, *real* or not. Whether or not others believe it, it's still your reality. These Support References will be Personal, Second Hand or Imagined, usually a combination of all three. Here's an example: You know you're a great fighter. How? You generally smoke most of your competition (Personal), your coach and training partners tell you how awesome you are, you see it in the write ups and on video (all Second Hand), and finally you see it in your head (Imagined). You dream of being the best, you play the mental pictures over and over in your mind's eye of outstanding future performances (Imagined). These references support your frame of belief to help bring you one step closer to being the best. This powerful triadic support drives you confidently, boldly and unerringly toward your victory again and again. But,

45

sometimes our mind creates conflicts of reference, and establishes conflicting beliefs. And sometimes those conflicts create a feeling of uncertainty. What do I mean? Have you ever driven your car out of your driveway with your parking brake on? You're accelerating, but there is resistance from the brake and you can feel it holding you back. That's what conflicting beliefs do… create resistance!

Avoiding Conflicts

I've seen athletes who usually do well, blowing through the competition, suddenly put that emergency brake on. There's a term in psychology for this known as "Approach Avoidance." With a fighter, it could be that he/she has been successful and on track, and something or someone influences their belief that they will succeed. In many cases, their imagination does the rest, creating a disruption in their direction and yanking the emergency brake on, so to speak. Another possibility is that they feel they are not worthy of the success they are achieving or that people won't treat them the same, if they become too successful. Other times it may be because they have a conflict in their values. I want to become great, but have seen what's happened to fighters that have been on that road. That's not who I am or want to become. These are all valid concerns. The question is, "What's most important to you?"

"To be a great champion you must believe you are the best. If you're not, pretend you are." - Muhammad Ali

Mental Exercise #1

Here's a great exercise to help confirm your beliefs. Draw three ovals on a page side by side in the Journal Entry area in the back of the book. Above that write your belief about something pertaining to you, your training, an event you're involved in, your skill sets, etc. Now, write in the ovals Personal, Second Hand and Imagined. Starting with the first oval-Personal References, draw a line to another oval and write an example (reference) you've personally experienced in the past that proves you are capable and have accomplished something similar. Next, draw another line with another bubble and continue your list, creating as many bubbles as you can. Next draw a line as you did previously, now for the Second Hand References. Who's told you "you can do this", where have you seen it done before, who else has done this? Find as many examples as possible. Last, draw a similar line and bubble connecting to Imagined (references). Here write what you see in your head, how do you see yourself succeeding? What do you imagine yourself doing absolutely excellent? Imagined References are the most powerful! Think of an instance in history where there were no Personal or Second Hand References, yet people still accomplished amazing feats, feats accomplished in exploration, science and human rights. Imagination ruled those references in the heads of pioneers.

Substantiating Your Beliefs

According to my friend Greg Nelson, who is an amazing trainer, currently known for developing the talents of several outstanding competitors in Combat Sports, with his most recent fighter being Brock Lesner. "The belief in those around (training partners especially) is huge. If a fighter feels his training partners abilities and skills are second to none in preparing him for an upcoming fight, his confidence is definitely heightened." Greg has long been driven by his powerful beliefs and emulates what it takes to be a champion at his academy in Minnesota.

I worked with a fighter once who had five consecutive wins, yet as his next fight neared I could sense he was very unsure. After talking to him, it was evident he was focusing not on the previous Personal References, but rather Second Hand References of what he had heard about this next competitor. Then his imagination took over, and apprehension seeped in. I recognized the problem immediately. His focus was on what he'd heard about the other guy, not what he'd done personally to his last five opponents. Once he realized I was right, his face changed immediately to confident and calm. Two days later he KO'd the guy in less than a minute. Most of the time your beliefs will be relative to what you focus on. Bottom line, if you look, you will find enough evidence to substantiate your belief and then move in the direction as if it were true.

Reframe Your Outlook

When Goliath came against the Israelites,
the soldiers all thought, "He's so big we can never kill him."
But David looked at the same giant and thought,
"He's so big, I can't miss him."
-DALE TURNER

What is reframing? Reframing is a method of changing the way we may look at something by placing it in another frame of perception to a person's viewpoint about the subject, changing the meaning and there by changing the emotion attached to the previous view or frame of reference. Our emotions are dramatically affected by the meaning we give to our experiences, and the meaning we give to any experience is shaped by the lens or filter through which we perceive it. The quote from Dale Turner is an awesome example of the power of reframing. Whereas the other soldiers all were afraid of Goliath's mammoth presence, David saw the situation in another, entirely different way. His frame of reference enabled him to feel powerful instead of petrified. After all, what we will do in any given moment depends not as much on our ability, as on our **state of mind**. Reframing is an invaluable tool for creating a Winning Mind Set. It gives you the opportunity to see things in different, more empowering perspectives.

Thomas Edison offers a classic example of reframing. It took him something like 10,000 attempts to invent the incandescent light bulb. When others chided him for failing so many times, and asked when he was going to give up his crazy idea, he was reported to have said, "I didn't fail, I just figured out another way *not* to invent the light bulb." He reframed what others saw as failure into a new distinction. He saw it as gaining more knowledge because he now knew one more approach that did not work, and so he could save time and effort by avoiding going in that particular direction. Because his reframing made him feel empowered and excited, he persevered. Had he been discouraged because he had failed yet again, chances are high that he would not have had the motivation to continue.

"The strongest leverage for all achievement is passion and desire. Weak desires, bring weak results, strong desires produce powerful results. The most difficult person to stop is the person with a burning desire"
- Kevin Seaman

Mental Exercise #2 How can **you** reframe a situation? Easy, all that you have to do is ask different questions. Consider the following in regard to any recent issue you may have experienced: *How might this be seen in a positive way? How can I use this constructively? What is actually good about this that I may not see, may be overlooking? In what ways does this get me closer to my goal? What did I learn from this that I could use in the future? What did I learn about myself? What lesson can I take from this? How will this experience make me better?*

Be sure to write your results down in the back of the book in the Journal Entry area, this helps materialize your thoughts.

"Everything we are at this very moment in time, is a result of each and every decision we have made in our life up until NOW. If we don't like the answer, time for us to ask better questions." –Kevin Seaman

When a fighter loses, it is essential for him to process the event mindfully. The challenge that many have is that they look into the future and project their current failure. So instead of feeling down only about their current result, they project it to include all future results. Their internal self talk might go something like this: "If I messed up here, and I've done it before, I'll probably do it again or I can't believe I keep doing this. I'll never get any better, I don't even know why I even bother…" One objective of reframing is to limit the emotion of "failure", which may include feelings of guilt, frustration, apprehension, and dejection, to the present experience only so that this negative emotion is not projected into the future. The other objective of reframing is to change the meaning you may have of the current experience from a negative, disempowering one, into a positive, empowering one; from a feeling of "I can't believe I screwed up so badly," to "I just learned what not to do in that situation." Be truthful with yourself, what do you need to work on next? Who can help you who is extraordinary at this skill? Get to work! Using reframing to focus and direct your emotions into positive change creates a Winning Mind Set, and motivates you to continue to strive towards reaching your goals.

"If we change our frame of reference by looking at the same situation from a different point of view, we can change the way we respond in life. We can change our representation or perception about anything and in a moment change our (emotional) states and behaviors."
– Anthony Robbins

One of the best examples of reframing I've ever heard came from World Renowned BJJ Black Belt John Machado during a class I was taking at the Inosanto Academy in Los Angeles. It went something like this, "When you tap, do not think of it as giving up. When you tap, you are thanking your partner. Thank you for showing what I need to work on, thank you for showing me not to get into that position again, thank you for helping me to learn. Thank you my friend"

"When you believe and think I can, something extraordinary happens. You activate a part of your brain called the Reticular Cortex. This small human bio-instrument immediately begins searching for all the possible ways for you to be successful. This creates drive, motivation, commitment and excitement. These qualities all directly relate to your success and the opportunities will disclose themselves!"
-Kevin Seaman

Lesson Six
The Power of Failure

"Our FEARS do not stop death, they stop LIFE"
-Rickson Gracie

The mere mention of the word FAILURE for some people creates an emotional knot that is tied to a conclusion of pain and anxiety. When we think of our past failures, there can be a powerful association, an association that creates a visual program of irretrievable loss, a finale, an ending. But, for me failure is actually an amazingly useful tool. It is, in my observation exactly what you perceive it as, and I'm proud to say, "I've failed miserably many times, before rising to success.

According to "Success Principles" expert, Jack Canfield, E+R=O or The *event* plus your *response* to that *event* equals your *outcome/results*. What that means is for every event, your outcome will be determined by your response. As one of my best coaches used to tell me, "Kevin, if you don't like the answer, maybe you need to ask a better question!" I know this may seem incredibly simplistic, but if you didn't get the outcome you expected, then it is very likely due to your response to the event (question) that took place.

"I have not failed. I've just found 10,000 ways that won't work." -Thomas Alva Edison

If you make your way through life without experiencing any real failure on a regular basis, you are in essence, a true failure! If you haven't strived for excellence, you've stayed safely in the harbor of mediocrity, never pushed beyond your comfort zone, or risked the extraordinary. This concept is what has driven me to train relentlessly in multiple combative arts for the past 40 years, drove me to train Professional Fighters, ski big mountains, and take up kitesurfing at age 50, when most of my peers are content to confine their adventures to the golf course or watching sports on TV. The fear and danger of stepping outside their comfort zone prevents them from feeling the exhilaration and rush of mixing it up on the mat, cutting an edge on beautiful Rocky Mountain slope or popping a lift on the warm Caribbean Sea.

Metaphorically, in strength training, it is the ability to push to FAILURE, that is the instrumental pivotal point of our success toward greater strength. If we only train with the weight that is manageable for us to succeed with, we will always remain at the same level of strength and proficiency.

"You are the way you are because that's the way you've accepted. No one has forced you to be WHO you are. If you really wanted to be any different, you would be in the process of changing right now, moving in the direction to where you really want to be"-Kevin Seaman

The Irrefutable Key

In order for us to succeed in the first place, we must possess (in most cases) a certain level of ability to accomplish what we set out to do. However, most people don't fail because they lack the skills or aptitude to reach their objective, they fail because they simply don't believe they can succeed. Their limiting beliefs determine their outcome. Our belief in ourselves in reference to success and failure is the irrefutable KEY to our outcome. What you believe with emotion and conviction becomes your reality! If you see failure as an end, you have been defeated. If you see failure as a part of the natural progression toward success, you have the opportunity to use it to actually help you to succeed on a level beyond your wildest dream.

Five Golden Rules for Success

At this point you may wonder how you can improve your odds against failure? Here are my Five Golden Rules to help you to use failure as leverage for success.

#1 Recognize The Opportunity and Act

First and foremost, don't ever let the possibility of failing at something detour you from the opportunity of going for it! When the window of opportunity opens, assess and act. This is not to say that you must do something that would threaten your life or freedom to the extent that the failure would be negatively life altering. You must of course use your best cognitive judgment to determine the potential gains and losses and balance them logically. So, once you've made your mind up that you will indeed succeed, use the following mental performance tools to help outweigh your success to failure ratio.

#2 Know What You Want

Be specific at what you want to achieve, write it down in as much detail as possible, if time allows. Next, set a timeline for accomplishment. Most importantly, look into why you want to accomplish this. Purpose is always more powerful than outcome. If you have a big enough why, your mind will direct you to the best ways to achieve your objective.

#3 You Get What You Ask For

Talk to yourself constantly about what you're going to do, how you're going to do it, and when you will do it, Be specific, always tell yourself what you want in the positive, personal and present tense. Use terms like; "I am doing this", "I am stronger, I am a better athlete and I am a better technician." "Today I am the best I can be." I am better today, than ever before." I work toward excellence." These statements confirm what *you* want in *positive* terms *now*! Establish a clear and substantial belief of who you are and your objectives as a fighter. **Focus only on what you want,** never on what you don't want. Always remember, you become what you think about most of the time! What happens on the inside happens on the outside. Remember, according to research, you already talk to yourself nearly 50,000 times a day. Unfortunately, research also shows that 80% of what most people say to themselves is usually in the form of negative self-talk. Hey, I don't make this stuff up guys, so, be positive.

Work to constantly improve your explanatory style, the way you communicate with yourself and mentally process the things that happen to you. Your thoughts, self-talk and inner visions (visualizations) are electrochemical events that affect your performance on every level. Use your inner communication to support and drive you toward your accomplishment.

"Good, Better, Best, Never Let It Rest".....That is our training attitude at The Academy."
 -Greg Nelson/ World Class Martial Artist and Coach

#4 The Past Does Not Equal The Future, Visualize Your Outcome

Create your future from your future, not from your past. Visualize yourself performing just exactly how you want to perform, succeeding just exactly the way you want to succeed. Visualization was instrumental in the success of my GOAL to become a World Champion at full contact stick fighting in 1992 in the Philippines, where I competed as the oldest member fighting on the US Team. I saw myself defeat my opponents literally hundreds of times, pummeling them victoriously in my mind's eye.

Visualization is one of the most powerful forms of mental training. Did you know that your body has almost the identical neurological impulses when you visualize doing something as when you actually do it! It's true! It's proven! If you've never accomplished the objective before, no worries, you can **model** someone who has. Play the image in your head over and over of them doing what you want to succeed at then, see yourself doing the same exact thing. I have accomplished absolutely amazing things using this same concept, and so can you.

#5 Pay Attention To Your Results

Fifth, no matter what the outcome, take total responsibility for your results, successful or not. Be true to yourself. This is the only way you can feel the level of empowerment necessary to learn from the failures and soar past them toward your achievement. When you take responsibility for your actions, your integrity will support you in your endeavor. Stop making excuses for your actions and performance and be truthful in your assessment. The truth will reveal to you, without hesitation, all the areas necessary for improvement to reach your ultimate goal. 90 percent of all failures come from people who have a habit of making excuses.

"If you believe, then you have already taken the first step towards your achievement." -Rickson Gracie

The Bottom Line

One of the world's leading record holders for goals in hockey was once quoted saying, "You miss every shot you don't take." Yet, few realize that Wayne Gretzky missed more than 90 percent of his shots. What ever it is you want to accomplish, the most important step is ACTION. Many times people fail to take action, because they are afraid to fail. I have also failed at some things many more times than I've succeeded, and view failure as a very important part of the learning process and the progression to excellence. Make one of your core beliefs to use failure as a gauge to assess the degree of difficulty, and to help render the time and the skill necessary for your success. I personally realize that patience and persistence have assisted me in my accomplishments more often than skill and aptitude.

Once you adjust and reframe your perception of failure from one of finality, to the progression and natural process toward ultimate success that it is, you will embrace failure and not fear it.

"If you're not making mistakes, you're not trying hard enough."
- Vince Lombardi, football coach

Lesson Seven
The Trusting Mindset Of A Champion

"Trusting your intuition means tuning in as deeply as you can to the energy you feel, following that energy moment to moment, trusting that it will lead you where you want to go and bring you everything you desire."
-Shakti Gawain

Earlier this year there was a big rematch of Machida and Shogun on the line at UFC 113 in Montreal, I began to reflect on the qualities that make a person embrace the stress of high-level competition, and then use that inflective energy to drive them like a bullet to their mark. For Lyoto Machida, this rematch is an opportunity to confirm his position as Champion. For Mauricio "Shogun" Rua, it's redemption. After so much controversy in regard to the decision from the last encounter, both fighters must feel enormous pressure to outperform their opposition.

So, what types of things might go through your mind, when people say, you were robbed, or point to you as being clearly outperformed? Although, everyone has an opinion and your opinion does not mean you are right (or wrong), from the athlete's point of view, it still magnifies the STRESS to an incredible degree. Those voices in your head, those pictures that you make, and your future actions are absolutely affected. A person must have an undeniable and absolute belief in their skills and abilities to an extent that they operate on a level of super-conscious performance, with complete and total confidence in their outcome of victory.

As a Performance Coach, I have studied areas of psychology,

Neuro-Linguistic Programming and cognitive neuroscience in relation to human performance. What I have found is that these concepts, how to process stress and how to get better at tuning into your target, and turning down the unnecessary internal and external NOISE are becoming important qualities of optimal performance and winning.

This "super-conscious performance", is without conscious thought, switching off the cerebral cortex function of questioning and focusing only on the target of that particular moment in time. That target is…GO OUT And GET WHAT YOU WANT!

While studying these areas related to optimal human performance I came across Dr John Eliot, a Cognitive Neuroscientist and psychologist from Virginia, who has studied both of these important elements.

This area is what Dr. Eliot in his book, Overachievement, The New Model For Exceptional Performance refers to as The Trusting Mindset. We have all experienced this Trusting Mindset, it was when we were too young and small to **know** enough to realize any other way. When you are a kid and you want something, do you wait and analyze the best approach or route? Maybe for a split second, then you beeline straight for it and get it. You do this without hesitation, as NIKE states, you *JUST DO IT!*

"The Trusting Mindset is what you were in before you knew any better". –Dr. John Eliot

Eliot goes on to say that "the opposite of the Trusting Mindset is the Training Mindset." Although both are important, it is the Trusting Mindset that moves you without thought, determination and analysis, beyond the realm of the conscious or the sub-conscious. It just allows you to do what it is **you do** to get you where you've pre-decided you want to be. The Trusting Mindset utilizes closed loop processing, bypassing the cerebral cortex and engaging the sensory cortex to the motor cortex in a loop of neurological signals. This reactionary thinking is what occurs if someone tosses a ball to you, you don't think about the velocity, size or distance, you just catch it.

For a Martial Artist or Martial Athlete this is precisely what we want to occur. To react to the stress and attacks without analysis, to just "Be in the Moment." This super-conscious mind or Trusting Mindset has been referred to throughout history in many cultures. It has been called "instinct" or "intuition", it has been referred to as the "responsive mind", "gut feeling", and the Japanese have called it "Mushin" which actually translates to **"no mind"**!

In the state of NO MIND, there is an absence of logical thought and judgment, the person is totally free to act and react towards an opponent without hesitation and without disruption from cognitive thoughts. In this mindset, a person relies not on what they think should be the next move, but what they've trained as a natural reaction or what is felt intuitively. The mind is responsive and working at a high level and usually at a high speed. Your mind is not on "auto-pilot", it is totally engaged on "Super-pilot."

"When I am fighting I am keeping my mind empty for any expectations. I am waiting for something unique, completely new." -Rickson Gracie

Contrastingly, open loop processing relays the information from a sensory receptor (eyes, ears, touch, etc.) to the sensory cortex to the hippocampus of the brain, which transfers the impulse to the cerebral cortex first, which then supplies an analysis of the variables, possibilities and interpreting what we should do prior to sending the signal to your motor cortex, as well as other areas of the brain. This is of course, a simplistic explanation of our brain's function; the human brain consists of approximately 10 billion interconnected nerve cells with innumerable extensions.

"The less effort, the faster and more powerful you will be."
-Bruce Lee

Cut To The Chase
The bottom line of this idea is to use the Training Mindset to train and the Trusting Mindset to perform. We all use the Trusting Mindset every day, when we do things like driving to work, eating, opening a door, etc.
The Training Mindset helps you to prepare yourself, get stronger, organize your approach, strategize your attack strengths, and analyze your opponent's weakness. But, it interferes with your actual performance.

What Do I Really Have Control Over?
We have the illusion that we have control over many facets of our lives, however the reality is, we only have control over three things. Once again, let me clarify this central principle I learned from Jack Canfield. There are only three things that we actually have control of in our lives.
1) **The things we say to ourselves, our inner dialog.**
2) **The pictures we make in our head, our visualizations.**
3) **Our response to our challenges; in effect, our actions.**
These three areas are crucial to our development as an athlete. They allow us to reflect on our training, our path

and ultimately our preparation for performance. Some of the BEST coaches I've studied agree, focus on your performance, and then just do what you've trained to do. Don't let the thought process interfere with your outcome.

An analogy John Eliot uses to illustrate this is that, to perform in the moment using the Trusting Mindset is similar to thinking like a squirrel. A squirrel lacks the cerebral cortex that we possess. So, as the squirrel runs across a power line, they don't analyze the dangers, they just point themselves at their target (the next pole) and GO! They, by definition have the perfect "closed loop" process mastered by default.

Mastering The Trusting Mindset
When people ask me, how can I learn to improve the power in my kick or sharpen my hand speed and striking skills? I answer…to get better at something you need to do more of it. In my book, **The Winning Mind Set**, I point out the 4 levels of learning, with the last being "Unconscious Competence." This is the point where you are just doing it, without conscious thought to impede your performance. To get to this point, you must sustain the point of "Conscious Competence" (the 3rd stage) until the skills transcend beyond being consciously driven. **In other words, you've got to have sick skills!**

Here's how it goes.
The process of learning a skill is for the most part gradual and repetitious as we pass through four evolving levels of competence.

The first level is known as "unconscious incompetence." This is the primary stage where you have no foundation. You are totally unaware that you lack a certain skill or ability.
The second level is "conscious incompetence." At this

level, you lack a particular skill or ability, but know it. You are conscious of your lack of skill. You may even want the desired skill very badly, yet are not able or prepared to invest the time necessary to move beyond this level.

The third level is "conscious competence." This is the level where you are well aware of you ability and proficient at it. The challenge is MOST people stop progressing, never transcending beyond this stage. They simply quit, believing they have gotten to the summit of their skill level.

The final stage is "unconscious competence", a level where you do whatever it is in a state of flow, without the struggle of conscious thought to impede your forward direction. You respond naturally in an excellent fashion. You perform as you are at that moment, a skilled technician without reflection. This is the state that every great musician, athlete, technician, etc. must reach to be exceptional. You just do it!

In order to get better at releasing yourself from the analytical albatross of thinking while performing, put your self in the position of operating from the Trusting Mindset during training. Use it when sparring, drilling, and doing cardio and endurance training. Try to use it more often than the Training Mindset, and it will become a super-conscious pattern.

Embracing Stress

When faced with stressful situations (like a championship fight, for Machida and Rua) or any challenging performance, many of us do our best to manage that stress. We try to do it by controlling our breathing or thinking relaxing thoughts, trying our best to put us out of this stressful state. Trying our darnedest to manage that stress. Attempting that is actually fighting against what is occurring naturally inside us. Since the dawn of the ages, mankind has developed a way of preparing themselves for battle, the hunt or fleeing from danger by using this remarkable biochemical change to help us survive. Our body is preparing us for the stress by increasing our heart rate, creating adrenaline, converting glycogen into needed glucose and drawing the blood from our stomach area to our muscles. We feel sensations like butterflies, irritability and the need to yawn to take on more oxygen. This is our body preparing us for battle. Instead of trying to manage the stress, we need to reframe our interpretation of what the stress means to us and reinterpret how we can **use** it. Embrace the stress, understand it and welcome it.

"A Brave heart is a powerful weapon, stay brave my friend."-Erik Paulson

Lesson Eight
The Crucial Role Our Values Play In Our Success

"Be yourself. There are some things that you can do better than anybody. Listen to the inward voice and bravely trust where it takes you."
-Kevin Seaman

It's your night! You are ready! Ready to compete in MMA at the highest level you ever have before. You mentally assess everything that has led you to this stellar moment in your competitive history. You're there because of your record and past performance. The show is set, the competitor is set, you are prepared physically and you are in the BEST shape of your life. You've put in the work and it's time. It would seem as though nothing can stand in your way. Your coach has reinforced that you're the better fighter. After all, you have the better striking, you're a more experienced wrestler, and your ground game is peak. But, in the back of your mind, you start to ask yourself questions. "What's the next step? Where will I go from here? How will I be viewed if I continue to smoke every opponent I meet? I mean, that's a good thing, right? Will my buddies still treat me the same? I've seen how some fighters handle success, recognition and the money that comes with it; will I end up like that? Is that really me?"
Or… "How will my coach and the guys I train with view me if I lose?" What if I let my team down? This is what I've worked for. I really can't lose this! What about my sponsors? I hate letting people down. I hate failure! I really need to

WIN this! This type of conflict can paralyze a competitor sub-consciously. Although they may want to win, they are also unsure of what success may bring. And sometimes competition just doesn't have the same meaning; it just doesn't feel like it did when they began competing. All of these factors make it FEEL as though they are being pushed in and pulled from different directions, like reversing the polarity on two magnets. Since the beginning of the sciences of philosophy and psychology, people like Aristotle knew the powerful motivating factors of moving away from PAIN and moving toward PLEASURE. The very meaning of the word motivation is "to move." Defined as an internal factor that induces behavior and gives a direction, motivation is integral to every athlete's life.

The reality is, this parallel of opposite forces influences us all. Some people are motivated more by avoiding what they perceive as pain; we refer to this as "moving away from." A simple example of this is, "I will not be defeated by this person." In this instance, the pain, frustration and possible humiliation of losing to someone they may not respect or feel is worthy in this their eyes, is a huge motivation, driving them toward their WIN. They move away from the pain of losing. Others are much more motivated by what they believe they will receive from achieving their goal, they are categorized as a "moving toward" personality. They are much more motivated by moving toward what they want, they see it in front of them, and they move toward the excitement, feeling of victory and success of their achievement. Although we are all motivated by both moving away from and moving toward, it is usually one that will motivate us more, depending on our personality. One of my favorite quotes by Fedor is a prime example of moving away from pain as a tremendous motivation for him.

"Years ago we hardly had anything to eat. Now I earn more money and I see every opponent as a man that tries to put me back to that poorer period. That man has to be eliminated." -Fedor Emelianenko

It's All About Your Values

As I've illustrated, these two aspects of pain and pleasure create a push/pull element in the behavior of every human being, determining what we will or will not do. This pain/pleasure principle is an emotionally driven action, based on feeling, our emotions and ultimately, our VALUES.
So, how do our values provide a powerful motivating force for our behavior? Well, our values are literally based on the emotions that we value. I mean, think about it. We all desire to have pleasure in our lives. Why do we want to WIN anyway? Because of the feeling we gain from winning. The reality is, we don't really want to be champion, we don't want the jobs, relationships, homes, and cars...we want the emotions that these things will bring us, we want the feelings we VALUE and believe these things will give us. These "things" are just a means to gain these emotional feelings. However, it is also useful, indeed vital, to understand what we also link pain to. Just as we all link varying degrees of pleasure to values, we also link varying degrees of pain to emotional states such as rejection, loneliness, failure, jealousy, and so on. These emotional states are ones we try to avoid, so I call them Avoided States. Bottom line? We all link pleasure to our values, and pain to avoided states. Many times, people identify their values and set goals to link up with these desired states, acting as if pleasure is the only driving force in a person's life; anything feared or avoided

is almost not to be spoken about. Still, looking at pleasures is only part of the equation. Unless you are aware of what a person also links pain to, it is difficult to help motivate them.

"Our greatest enemies, the ones we must fight most often, are within." -Thomas Paine

Typically, if someone has a mixed pain/pleasure association toward what something means to him or her, you see a behavior we call in psychology "Approach – Avoidance." That is where someone has an initial attraction for something or someone, but then pulls back because a part of them does not want it. In Martial Athletics approach-avoidance is very common. A motivated athlete wants to compete, they train hard for it, they sacrifice, they tell people, they visualize themselves doing it, but when the time is near, they may become tentative. Many times this is a mixture of nervousness, self-imagery, self-concept and ego. Nervousness is normal in extreme sports. It is actually part of the physiological and psychological process of self-preparation we go through prior to anything that is difficult, dangerous, and combative or life threatening. I believe if there isn't an element of nervousness, then...
A) You may not be taking this seriously, which can be dangerous. Or...
B) It's really not an extreme sport!

"Failure is the tuition you pay for success."
-Walter Brunell

The KEY is learning how to control and utilize that nervousness. Self-imagery and self-conception are personality components. Self-imagery is how you see yourself visually, internally…are you skilled enough, able, worthy, etc. Where as self-concept is who you think you are. I've always believed that in order to become successful you cannot fear failure. If you fail, you have accomplished a natural step in your progress to succeed. So, if you are hurt by the mere possibility of failure, it will loom in your sub-conscious and create cracks in your image of yourself and who you "think you are." Egocentricity is the single most powerful killer of dreams, aspirations and goals! It appears as a little voice inside saying, "What if?….

I Want To, But I Can't

To get a better understanding of these concepts, lets look at how this works in other areas of life as I illustrate some examples of "Approach – Avoidance." Someone wants a promotion (he values success, feelings of accomplishment, freedom due to a higher income, and making a difference), yet may not want it at the same time (avoided states being a belief that he will spend more time at work and less with family, which equates to feeling loss of love, closeness, pressure; perhaps he feels like he would have to alter relationships with co-workers, and links this to a feeling of superiority, something he wants to avoid, push/pull) A salesperson wants to be successful, but fears rejection; an athlete has a desire to improve, but fears failure; a person wants to make new friends, but fears that he or she won't know what to say (humiliation, nervousness, awkwardness). Get the idea? In fact, I've had some athletes tell me they love to fight, but get feelings of awkwardness, feeling uncomfortable during press interviews, and in front of the crowd when they first step into the cage or the ring. It is useful, then, even critical that you take into account both sides of the pain / pleasure scale when helping yourself or others to be successful in any endeavor.

How Can I Use This?

To better understand what this means to you and your performance, think of your Values and Your Avoided Sates as two sides of a scale, with your GOAL as an MMA Competitor in the center fulcrum of the scale. Write your goal in the space below.

Your Goal: _____

Values	Avoided States
_____	_____
_____	_____
_____	_____
_____	_____
_____	_____

Next...

Take a moment and reflect on your top five values in relation to your sport.

Now, list them, then, ask yourself, "If I could only retain one value, which would be most important to me?" Next ask what your next most important value you could retain would be? Go through your list of values, using this same method to designate a list of five prioritized values in a hierarchy. Got it? Now do the same for your Avoided States. Ask yourself, "What would you most like to avoid in competition? When you think about your most negative memories or visualizations, this emotion kept popping up. Is this then, the emotion you would most like to avoid? If you could never feel these five emotions again, which five would they be? Which four, three, two and one? Great, now you have your list of your avoided states in a prioritized hierarchy. Examine your list of emotions side by side and notice if there are any conflicts that may exist between the pleasure and pain states within your values hierarchy?

Create a list of *Values* on one side of a page, and *Avoided States* on the other side. Then review it closely and see if anything is missing. States can always be added, so be careful about taking any off at this point since sometimes we judge ourselves (we *shouldn't* feel that way, or we really *should* feel this way).

Values Avoided States

Conflicts between valued states and avoided states are very common, and in fact are natural. There is an inherent dynamic tension between these two. If you value peace, then you try to avoid conflict; if you value love, then you most likely avoid hate; if you value success, you try to avoid failure. But if you are going to have success, you will experience failure. Do you recall it took Thomas Edison nearly 10,000 attempts before he succeeded at the light bulb? Many people do fail, but they don't allow their failures, their feelings of failure, or their fears of failure to stop them. That is the difference.

"If necessity is the mother of invention, then failure must be its father." -Steve Young

Let's stay with these examples of success and failure, because you will certainly deal with this both with yourself and others. Any person who wants to be successful in anything, you name it, and he or she will fail far more times than they will succeed. Riding a bike, we all fell down far more times than we succeeded in staying up at first. Learning to walk, did you ever see a baby "get" walking on his first try? Conversely, did you ever see a baby get so frustrated and angry because he didn't walk perfectly that he quit? That he gave up and never tried again because he hadn't gotten it yet? Of course not, but have you ever seen non-babies do that? Not you personally, but maybe people you know?

Many people value success, but they also want to avoid feelings of failure (or feeling like a failure). The problem comes when a person's fear or avoidance of failing prevents him from taking action and trying, or going through the necessary repetition of trial and error that it takes to master something. You'll never get where you want to be by focusing on what you fear. You must focus on what you value rather than on what you want to avoid. One of my favorite coaches once told me, "Kevin, your mind can only focus on one thought at a time. It can switch back and forth, but, ultimately you can't think two things simultaneously, you are… either smart or stupid, strong or weak, successful or a failure, in your mind, you either suck or you don't. You can't hold more than one thought at a time. You are either this or that, not both at the same time. So, choose wisely which one thought you want to hold on to."

All external events are inherently neutral until you respond mentally and assign an emotional context to them. Almost 90% of all fears are imaginary. They are a product of your mind and do not exist in reality.

We all Play By Rules
Take a moment to reflect and review your list of hierarchies and rules, this may help to trigger your thought processes by asking some of the following questions:
1) As you look at your list of values and avoided states, is

the order consistent with WHO you want to be?

2) If not, how would you change the order? What impact would that have on you? What things do you think you would start doing? What things would you no longer do?

3) As you look at your list of rules, to what extent do they support you in "winning" according to your values?

4) To what extent might your rules hold you back, or prevent you from winning?

5) If appropriate, how might you change your rules to be more consistent with your values and avoided states hierarchy?

6) How would any of these changes impact your life / performance / attitude?

Next time you feel awkward about doing something, look at WHY you may struggle or feel unmotivated about doing it, and if this event could potentially cause you to feel tremendous anxiety, shame or possibly failure. Your tentative approach may not be as important as WHY you feel this way. Do you choke on "Fight Night", yet soar in practice? Do you feel great when competing against your subordinates, but feel anguish when the competition is real? Look deep as to the WHY, seek to understand your actions, and then unleash the power of letting go of your fear, and as Nike suggested, **"JUST DO IT !"**

"Be more concerned with your character than your reputation, because your character is what you really are, while your reputation is merely what others think you are."
-John Wooden, basketball coach

Lesson Nine
Hit The Center Of The Bull's Eye

"Ability is what you're capable of doing. Motivation determines what you do. Attitude determines how well you do it."
- Lou Holtz

What pushes you to achieve greatness? What creates that drive you need in order push forward, regardless of obstacles, to accomplish the goals you hold in your heart? What is the motivation? The word motivation comes from the Latin phrase "to move forward" or reason to move forward. So, what is it that motivates you, moves you forward? As we have hit the end of 2010 and begin a new year, we should think about our GOALS and what we will accomplish as we move forward in the future as a fighter or coach, and in every area of our life!

In this lesson I will teach you the approach to goal attainment that has worked for me. **Take 5 minutes to read this and take the action in your life and you will never, ever be the same.**

In The Cross Hairs

What is a Goal? A goal is like a target really. If you currently have clear, written goals to lead you forward, you are part of a very unique and elite group. You are aiming at the center of the bull's eye of your target. You are in the top 3% of people who have high aspirations about their personal achievement. It's true, according to the experts less than 3% of North Americans have written, specific, detailed goals. Not only that, about 10% have goals committed to memory. This would

78

be like aiming at the outside rim of your target. Committing goals to memory is not an adequate way to clearly focus on your objective. What about the remaining 87%? Well, they have no goals at all. But, why are goals so important in the first place?

"One day Alice came to a fork in the road and saw a Cheshire cat in a tree. "Which road do I take?" she asked. "Where do you want to go?" was his response. "I don't know," Alice answered. "Then," said the cat, "it doesn't matter."-Lewis Carroll, author

My all time favorite coach Brian Tracy once told me, "If you don't know where you're going, any road will take you there!" Most people don't really know which road to take, simply because they don't have a clear picture of their destination. Without a destination, it's so easy for us to fall into the trap of complacency. To be content, just getting by day to day, without pushing to achieve the things we really want to change in our lives or succeed at. We may rationalize why we can't succeed by using negative self-communication, telling ourselves we don't have the skills, resources, knowledge, and education or time it takes to achieve what we want.

First, it's not knowledge and education that makes people succeed. The world is full of skilled, educated, knowledgeable failures. People who succeed at anything have some very specific methods they utilize to accomplish their objective. **But, first and foremost, you must know your objective or goal.**

People who succeed are those who…

1) Know <u>specifically</u> what they want! They have a specific goal or set of goals they want to achieve. So, write your goals down and be <u>specific</u>; the more detailed, the better. Something truly amazing happens when you write down your goals. It's as if they are beginning to actually process in your mind the moment your pen hits the page. Designate a target date or time period to accomplish those goals; place your written goals where you can see them daily.

2) Have developed the ability to take consistent <u>action</u>. In other words, they will consistently do what it takes to succeed. Self-discipline, attitude, personal beliefs and values all play a major role in motivating us to take action toward our achievements. It is not your intentions, but rather it is your actions that will allow you to succeed. To yet again quote that famous slogan, "Just Do It!"

3) Have persistence. They <u>don't give up!</u> Every person you see who has achieved greatness has failed over and over to finally succeed. There are few unrealistic goals, only unrealistic time frames to accomplish them. Losers quit when they're tired; winners quit when they've succeeded.

4) Learn from the end-results. If the approach they took didn't work, they adjust their approach again and again until they get the results they want. Let me use an analogy to expand this idea. When I lived near the ocean, I used to sail whenever I had the opportunity. When a sailboat leaves a harbor in pursuit of a destination, it sets its compass in the direction of its objective. But in the course of travel, as the boat is challenged by the currents, the wind and the weather, the captain will need to change the boat's direction and adjust the approach in order to succeed and reach his destination. Be flexible in your approach. **You** are the captain of your destination.

"The law of harvest is to reap more than you sow. Sow an act, and you reap a habit. Sow a habit and you reap a character. Sow a character and you reap a destiny."
–James Allen

Develop The Muscle

One of the best ways to begin with goal setting as a habit is to work from a list on a daily basis. Here are a few tips on using a list to increase your productivity and develop your goal setting muscles.

1) Work from a list every day. Update your list for the next day the night before or first thing in the morning. Write it down! Something amazing will happen when you materialize your thoughts on to paper.

2) Hold fast to your "standard procedure" of working from your list, refusing to do anything that is not on the list. This is accomplished by updating your list as you work through your day.

3) Evaluate tasks by deadline. Whenever possible work on your largest or most difficult, least favorite task first. This will ensure it gets done, not ending up on the next day's list. If you insist on completing the smaller tasks first you will make little headway. Small tasks will continue to appear as your day unfolds.

4) Evaluate your tasks for value and return. Which task will bring you the most return on your effort? ***One whale is worth a thousand buckets of minnows!***

5) By working from a list everyday you will accomplish more in a week than most people do in months or even years.

6) Remember there is no such thing as unreasonable goals, just unreasonable time frames.

"I just want to be known as the best ever, is that too much to ask?" -BJ Penn

Ready, Aim...Fire!
I write my goals in a small hardbound journal. Use what you feel is best for you.

1) What do you want?
Write it down clearly and in complete detail. This is the "*What*" pertaining to your goals.
Example: I will compete in five Pro MMA events in 2012, being in the best shape of my life and performing to the best of my ability. I will develop my MMA skills by continuous, regimented daily training in the following areas: **Stand up-**
footwork, individual striking w/ all tools, combination skills in Muay Thai. **Transition/ground-** *positioning/angling, clinch, takedowns, submission, escapes/counters, G&P.* **Attribute qualities-** *timing, power, strength, flexibility, focus cardio and muscular stamina, dietary discipline, and mental training.*

2) Make an "Action Plan" of everything you need to do to over the next few days, weeks, months get you closer to your goal. This is the "*How*".

3) Organize your list in terms of activities pertaining to time and priority. What's first, what's most important? Next you need to set your deadlines and several sub-deadlines. This is the "*When*"

4) Why is this important to you? What would it mean to you? In order to be successful we must create a meaning for what we do. How would accomplishing these goals affect your life and your future? It is usually who we

become while accomplishing our goals that is most important. This is the *"Why"*.

5) Take action toward your goal and begin immediately to do something to move you in the direction of your goal. What are you committed to do to take your first step forward?

GOAL SETTING EXERCISE
For the purpose of this exercise let's focus on the major athletic goals you would like to achieve in relation to MMA.

<u>**FIRST !**</u>
Decide what you want. <u>This is the most important step,</u> if you don't know exactly what you want in complete detail you'll never get it! Remember, if you don't know where you're going, any road will take you there.

What do you want? Write it down clearly and in complete detail. This is the *"What"* pertaining to your goals.
Make an "Action Plan" of everything you need to do to over the next few days, weeks, months get you closer to your goal. This is the *"How"*.
Organize your list in terms of activities pertaining to time and priority.

Start now on the page below!
What's first, what's most important? This is the *"When"*

1)_____
2)_____
3)_____
4)_____
5)_____

6)_____

7)_____

8)_____

9)_____

10)_____

Next you need to set your deadlines and several sub-deadlines. _____

_____

_____

_____

_____

_____

_____

_____

_____

_____

_____

Take action toward your goal and begin immediately to do something to move you in the direction of your goal. What are you committed to do to take your first step forward?

Lastly, why is this important to you? What would it mean to you? If you have a BIG enough "Why", then the "What" and "How" are much easier. In order to be successful we must create a meaning for what we do. How would accomplishing these goals affect your life and your future? It is usually who we become while accomplishing our goals that is most important. This is the "Why".

Direct 100% total commitment toward the accomplishment of your goal. Flexibility is absolutely crucial; if what you're doing isn't working, change your approach, if that doesn't work, change your approach again until you succeed.

"It is my opinion that developing a mindset of having clear, distinct, written GOALS and working toward these goals, daily and incrementally is the single most significant thing that will determine your ultimate success and absolute happiness in your life!"
-Brian Tracy

Tapping Into Your Sub-Conscious

Any person who wants to be successful in anything, regardless of what it is, he or she will fail far more times than they will succeed. Riding a bike, we all fell down far more times than we succeeded in staying up at first. Learning to walk, did you ever see a baby walk on his first try? Conversely, did you ever see a baby get so frustrated and angry because he didn't walk perfectly that he just quit? So frustrated that he gave up and never tried again because he hadn't gotten it yet? Of course not! But have you ever seen non-babies do that? Not you personally, but maybe people you know? Many people value success, but they also want to avoid feelings of failure (or feeling like a failure). The problem comes when a person's fear or avoidance of failing prevents him from taking action and trying, or going through the necessary repetition of trial and error that it takes to master something. Remember, we all move toward pleasure and away from pain. Some of us are driven more by moving toward pleasure, some more by away from pain.

Many times people set goals that have very little to do with what they truly value in life, or they set goals that do not take into account what they want to avoid. Then they wonder why they aren't following through, and label themselves as lazy or undisciplined, that's rarely the case. Usually, the problem is that people's goals have nothing to do with their value system or how they like to be reinforced.

"Progress is not quick or easy, it is the process of your personal improvement that develops WHO you are, NOT the destination at which you work to arrive at. Embrace the process. That's where the true genius lies." –Kevin Seaman

There is a unique cycle that occurs when we predicate goals that are in alignment with our values. As we work toward our value driven objective we feel totally natural in our pursuit and once this goal is achieved, our values are satisfied and supported by our accomplishment. Therefore our goals support our values and our values in turn support us in the direction of our goals. **At this point you may say,.. "That's great, Kevin"…but**

How can I use this? Here's how! Get some leverage. Think of the goal or objective you wish to achieve, but have had difficulty completing. Make a clear picture of this goal in your head. Now, think of how great you would feel, when this goal was completed. Think of all the benefits you would gain and the feeling of total satisfaction knowing that you have accomplished this. Visualize yourself with a huge smile on your face, as you finish. Got that picture clear and complete in your mind's eye. GOOD! Now, think of the negative emotions associated with not completing this same task. Think of the frustration you've experienced now and before as this goal once again slips away from your grasp. Think of how you will feel in the future as you embrace the loss of satisfaction and negative drain these emotions have, as you face the reality that you failed only because you have given up! Run these two mental videos over and over in your head. These visions are the carrot and the stick. Now, write "The Carrot and the Stick" on a small note pad and put the note somewhere conspicuous, somewhere you will see it daily for at least one week. When you see it run your mental video. In a short time you will begin to change your association to this goal and connect your emotional content via your values and the principle of pain and pleasure. I've had amazing results with this, and if you believe it, and try it, so will you.

You'll never get where you want to be by focusing on what you fear. Instead focus on where you want to be. Focus on what you want and work toward it's accomplishment and enjoy the best of success in your near future!

"I have missed more than 9,000 shots in my career. I have lost almost 300 games. On 26 occasions I have been entrusted to take the game-winning shot... and I missed. I have failed over and over and over again in my life. And that's precisely why I succeed." – Michael Jordan

"The difficulty most people have with challenges is due to FOCUS! When you focus on the PROBLEM your mind asks 'Why can't I ?' A simple shift to focusing on the SOLUTION, and immediately your mind asks 'How can I? ' Work to become Solution Oriented, rather than Problem Focused!"
- Kevin Seaman

Lesson Ten
5 Keys for Exceptional Coaching

"The human body is a submission just waiting to happen"
-Erik Paulson

How To Be The Driving Force That Turns A Competitor Into A Champion
As a coach, you want to be on the cutting edge of your field. You strive to learn and integrate the newest technology in the field of speed, strength, conditioning and nutrition into your program. You study the cutting edge in striking, Jiu Jitsu, footwork and positioning. You may bring other coaches in to add another dimension to training. You work to develop the very best qualities in your individual fighters and team with the intent to escalate them closer to the summit of their potential. In addition, you've probably invested in, and then committed countless hours to study what the best coaches do, learning their methods, approaches, drills and progressions. You do everything to ensure the very best outcome. Or...do you?

Now, remember the question I asked in the very beginning of this book? I ask every athlete and coach this question. In competition, how much of the outcome is attributed to physical skill and how much is attributed to mental aspects? Usually the answer ranges from 50/50 to 80% mental and 20% physical. Then I ask them, what do you do to train the psychological side? 99% of the time they stare at me, searching for an answer. Now...you know the answer! If you haven't tapped into the mental side; you are at best, at

89

50% of your potential, and if you've made it this far in the book, you've realized how crucial Mental Training is to your success. Well, in reality, this same principle goes way beyond competition and into the improvement of performance in everything we do, including coaching!

The thing is, even if we have a degree in the field of Physical Education, we really aren't taught how to effectively apply mental performance tools in college. We studied the finer points of anatomy, physiology, kinesiology, and exercise science, and we make an effort to understand the strategic approaches and essentials of the sport we coach. But, other than a couple psychology classes in college, we simply aren't exposed to how to apply the base principles, let alone a comprehensive application of mental performance techniques we can actually use in athletics.

Here are **just a few** of the very best coaching methods I've had the great fortune to be exposed to over the past 30+ years as a national and world class athlete, trainer and coach. They are based on my dogmatic need to ask,

"That's great, how can I use this?"

Key #1
You Get What You Focus On

As I pointed out previously, there are only three things that we truly have control over: the things we say to ourselves, the pictures we visualize in our head, and the action we take. In the first key, I will outline the foundational principle of looking where we want to go and asking ourselves what we want, rather than what we don't want, and the role this has as a crucial point of internal focus for a winning mindset.

Let me illustrate this point. You get into a cab and the driver asks, "Where you going?" At that point you start telling him where you want to go. Then as he takes off you start giving him various conflicting directions sending him to locations totally unrelated to where you first asked him to go. SOUNDS RIDICULOUS, doesn't it?

Yet, many times we do the same exact things to ourselves. Instead of telling ourselves what we are going to do or what we want, we tell ourselves what we don't want. When I do consulting work with athletes I always start out asking them what they want, what they would like to concentrate on as a focus when we are working together. I am amazed at how often they will then **tell me what they don't want.** In fact, usually they will begin by giving me a list of all the things they are deficient in and don't want to do or be anymore. The list will go something like this, I don't want to choke in the clutch, I don't want to miss the shot under pressure, I don't want to let my coach, team, parents, etc. down. I don't want to blow my big chance. I wish I wouldn't get so nervous when the score gets close, I wish I wasn't so slow, everybody's better at _____ than me. Why can't I perform in/on the ring, the cage, field, court, ice, etc., like I do in practice?

Did you know, that we have the most amazing built in homing device available, that there is only one other animal that has a goal seeking homing device that is as sophisticated and accurate as the one human beings posses? The homing pigeon is the only other being in the animal kingdom that even comes close. There is a part of our brain called the reticular cortex. This small finger size part of our brain is instrumental in filtering information, sort of a like a bouncer at a club that allows only certain clients to enter. This filtering system is known as the Reticular Activating System, a master sorting system that is truly invaluable to us. When you focus on something, your mind looks for every possible way to get it. So, always focus on what you want, not on what you don't want!

Remember that research I mentioned that has shown that people talk to themselves nearly 50,000 times per day? In fact, once again, you're talking to yourself right now. You're probably saying something like, "That's right! I do remember that " or "Yeah...OK?" Just as you talk to yourself, so do your fighters and this "self talk" is many times what directs us in our actions.

So, how can you use this?

What we say to ourselves prior or during competition or for that matter any situation that demands a high level of performance, is a major key to the success or failure of that performance. Here is a strategy for you to test. Ask your athletes what they do best, what are their individual key qualities? Next tell them to focus on those qualities and visualize themselves doing it exceptionally. Ask them to use their inner voice to confirm this over and over, then track the results.

Here's an example: I used this with a Mixed Martial Arts Pro I was coaching, "Nobody can stand with me, I can out strike them, and I know I am in better cardiovascular shape. They may be in as good of shape as me, but will never be in better shape. I can use my unique qualities (length, leverage, range and speed) to my advantage every moment I am in the cage. I will use these qualities to press my opponent constantly, throwing him into the defensive. **I am in control of this fight."**

Now, these are qualities this individual knows he possesses, as he focuses on them they become more real for him. He focuses on what he has, not on what he doesn't have. The outcome...at 19 years old, Tamdan "The Barn Cat" McCrory was 10-0 as a Pro with nobody ever going the distance with him and one of the youngest athletes to be signed by the UFC.

Key #2
If you don't like the answer, ask a better question.
Our minds are formulated to seek exactly what we ask
ourselves for. If you ask yourself, why can't I do this? Your
mind will find information to support all the different reasons
why you in fact, can't do it. For example as a fighter, if
you ask, "Why can't I knock this guy out?" Your mind will
support your conviction as to why, providing you with all
the reasons you can't, because that is what you asked for.
The profound reality is, we get what we ask for. Instead of,
what's the matter with me? A better question would be, how
can I improve these circumstances or how would someone
else approach this, modeling someone you hold in high regard
as a problem solver in that field or area? In 1996 my Thai
Boxing teacher Ajarn Chai held the focus mitts, as he does for
all his students one night at the Inosanto Academy. He held
what seemed to be endless rounds for his senior students, just
when I thought he was done, he said, "Oh, one more." He
looked at me and I jumped in the ring. For some reason, I was
extremely nervous and performed way below my potential.
Ajarn asked, "What was wrong?" My answer burst out of me,
"You make me nervous, Sir." He smiled and said, "No, Kevin.
You make yourself nervous!" That question and my answer
changed the way I looked at things immediately.Questions are
extremely powerful tools for changing our mindsets. Asking
questions can do three things. It can change what we focus
on, it can change what we delete, and it can give us access
to different resources (who, what, where, how, when) to help
achieve our desired ends. Questions can also help gain access
to feelings or emotional states very quickly, and as such, you
will want to become adept at asking excellent ones.

OK, now how can you use this one?

Let's put this to work from the perspective of offense. If you ask yourself, "Why can't I get this guy on the defensive?" your mind is problem focused. It becomes stuck in a loop of reasons "Why?" If however you ask, "How can I get this guy to become more defensive?" your mind makes a dramatic switch in it's distinction and now becomes solution oriented, looking for the ways it can solve the problem (question). Now, we've all been told spend 10% of our energy on the problem, and 90% on the solution. Search for the possibilities by asking possibility questions. If I were HIM how would I get around him, what are his strengths and weaknesses? What is he thinking? Who knows more about this (or this guy) than I do? What would BJ Penn, Georges St Pierre, Jon Jones or any iconic champion in my sport do? What am I missing in my approach? Will I drive this guy back on his heels in my first attempt, 2nd or 3rd? In order to accomplish this how do I have to think?

What do I have to say to myself? How do I have to move? Who do I have to become?

Key# 3
Raise The Standards

What got you here to this point will not get you to where you want to go. What do I mean by this? As a player, team, or coach, you are in a constant league of competitive improvement and evolution. You cannot play at the level that got you to the state championships, when you are in the nationals. You cannot play or think at the level you were at as an amateur fighting as a Professional. What got you here will not get you where you want to be. Now, this is not to say you should change your approach, if it works for you on the levels you are now competing at; then it is sound, in concept and principle. The KEY Component to focus on is the "elevation of the standards" you and your players hold for themselves.

That's Great, but how can I use this?

Ask yourself, am I a World Class Coach? If the answer is not absolutely affirmative, there is an issue with your self-concept. If the answer is yes, then how does a World Class coach act? Think? Dress? Stand? Speak? Interact? Are your standards as high as possible? Do you expect more from yourself than anyone else possibly could? If you are honest, you are thinking, "I have some work to do." And how about your fight team? Do they emit the energy of a team of Champions? Do they practice at the highest standards, play their very best, walk, talk and act with the confidence, style and charisma of a champion? Are they 100% ON when they practice, train and compete? Do they fight with the intent, desire and passion as if no one could possibly expect more out of them than themselves?

Key# 4
Improve The Self-Concept
This key also ties in with all the keys to transforming an athlete into a champion. It is our self-concept, our idea of who we are, or can be that makes up a large part of our personal identity. How we perceive ourselves, our concept of ourselves has a tremendous effect on the decisions that we make on a day-to-day basis. The term self-concept refers to those beliefs you have acquired that relate directly to you. Your self-concept determines the way you behave, and the way you perform at every activity. I have personally never witnessed an athlete whose performance could exceed his self-concept. The other major component is self-image, the mental picture you have of yourself. Your self-image sets the boundaries of your individual accomplishment. It defines what you can and

cannot be. If you expand the self-image, you expand the area of "the possible." The development of an adequate, realistic self-image will seem to permeate the individual with new capabilities, new talents, and literally turn failure into success. Remember, you are who you think you are!

How can I use this?

In order for us to have a clear distinction of our capability, aptitude and indeed our potential, we need to consider what our areas of strengths and weaknesses may be. When we have that critical combination of attributes, necessary to succeed in our chosen field of endeavor developed to a level outstanding to that of our competition, we increase our chances for success beyond what we would have ever believed possible! Our attributes can be both psychological and physical in nature and can be naturally adopted skills and traits, or specifically learned and cultivated.

Remember when I had you access your attributes and Critical Success Factors in Lesson Three? Well, now use it with the athlete you're coaching. Make a list of each area that your athlete has, as a "strength" and that which "needs improvement", both physically and psychologically. Discuss the list with them to be sure it is accurate. Then, define the critical success factors (CSF) this individual needs for their optimal performance in their sport or role. As the athlete reviews the CSF's, define the strength this person has and show them how this makes them unique as an individual. This helps them to focus on the qualities they possess and defines them as an important asset as a player/member, elevating their self-concept and self-image.

Key# 5
Belief In Outcome
This key is really the Master Key for all the previous four.

Belief is a feeling of certainty. There is no **maybe**, just certainty. So, how do we develop our beliefs? They happen and are proven to us by our references. These references come in the form of first hand (it actually happened), second hand (others told us, news, TV, etc.) and imagined. For some, what others believe is most powerful. For others it is based on real events. For many, it is what they imagine will happen that governs what they choose to believe. The bottom line is *"What we believe becomes our reality, and we don't live in reality, we live within our personal representation of reality."* This is why some people will compete at levels that astound us at times, then fold when they are put in a position that is incongruent with who they believe they are and the level they believe they can perform at. As a coach, you've seen it over and over.

You have an athlete with amazing potential and you find yourself wondering, "He's a great fighter, I'm just not sure **who's** going to show up when he gets here!" So, what can you do to change someone's belief? And if it's that powerful and controlling, can you really change it? Both are very good questions.

Let's look at how we can use this one. In order to change a belief we must adjust our references. Let's go back to Key# 1, you get what you focus on. This is what distinguishes the difference between a champion and everyone else. A champion focuses on the references they have in relation to excellence, they think about the positive references that relate to their personal experiences, what others have accomplished, said positively about them, etc., and most of all, they imagine success. They see it, feel it hear it and taste it. That is what they focus on and that is what they become. They make those images big,

bright and bold in their mind's eye constantly, and so it becomes. They push their thoughts and visions about their losses, failures and undesirable outcomes way back in the darkest file room, making them a small, unimportant learned test, that has expired in it's value, no longer part of the future. When I look to find an athlete's "sticking point", I always find it is in some way related to what they believe to be true. Is it always reality?…No, but it's always their reality.

One of the most coachable athletes I have ever had the opportunity to work with was Michael. Michael was an engineering student at Cornell University in the nineties. An avid soccer player, Michael had incredible hand/eye and hand/foot coordination. He was what I would term a physically intelligent individual. Michael studied Thai Boxing with me through his courses offered at Cornell and his private academy. I remember telling him, "If you ever decide to compete in Muay Thai, I can help you to become a champion. Once Michael had decided he wanted to try his hand at ring competition he committed himself entirely. I knew as I trained Michael that he was different than most of the people I'd trained for competition. Whatever Michael learned he absorbed and applied at a rapid rate. Michael's first bout went the distance. His second bout ended in 27 seconds with the opponent collapsed in the corner. In setting up his third bout I decided to give Michael a challenge. In order for me to confirm Michael's belief of his absolute success in his future outcome, I had to use a few techniques to leverage his commitment. When I discussed the next scheduled bout with Michael, I used Michael's association with what he had done so far. I then focused Michael's attention on what one of his sparring partners had accomplished. I also used contrast when explaining to Michael about his proposed opponent.

When Michael asked how many fights this individual had, I remarked with, "a few". "Michael his record doesn't really matter, you can beat him. Charlie beat him and you can hang with Charlie. You spar with Charlie all the time. Charlie knocked him out", I confirmed. I also used a series of anchoring techniques to help Michael prepare for the bout, as I did with all the competitors I train. During the bout Michael overwhelmed the more experienced opponent much to the shock of the crowd and the competitor's corner. When Michael came back to the corner he winked at me. This was a personal anchor Michael had developed. Michael listened attentively to my instructions and applied the strategies with flawless intent. After the bout Michael was the obvious victor. As things settled down Michael approached me and asked him what this individuals record was. "25 and 2 now Mike, why... I smiled? "Well sir, you told me he only had a few fights and someone told me that he was the undefeated Pennsylvania State Champion, " Michael said with a smile. "Not undefeated, Michael, Charlie knocked him out. Michael, I would have never put you in the ring with him if I thought you would have been outclassed. But, let me ask you a question? Would you have fought him if you'd known his exact record?" I asked. "No, I don't think I would have" Michael said, still grinning. Michael went on to win time and time again, including the New York Golden Gloves Championship in boxing and is now an accomplished mechanical engineer living in California, still training and teaching Muay Thai.

These keys are but a few ways to unlock the potential of your future champions. Being positive is important, but to accomplish anything it is **ACTION** that is the Golden Key to Success.

"No great performance ever came from holding back." *-Don Greene, performance coach*

Lesson Eleven
Simply To Simplify

*"Making the simple complicated is commonplace; making
the complicated simple, awesomely simple, that's creativity."*
- Charles Mingus

One of the most remarkably amazing qualities I have
witnessed in the truly gifted martial arts masters I have had
the opportunity to meet, observe or trained with, is their
focus on the foundational basics. They have a nearly flawless
execution of simplicity. This absolute and total understanding
of the quality of simplicity allows them to respond both
physically and psychologically to most problems with an
equally simple solution. In martial arts and martial athletics
competition, the more complex a defense or attack is, the
more likely it will be defended against. As well, the larger a
motion is the easier it is to counter, deflect and avoid. After
all, the easiest and most times, the best route between two
points is a straight line, right? When training with Professor
Relson Gracie, the second eldest son of the late Grandmaster
Helio Gracie, I was in awe of his extraordinary nature when
explaining and performing the simplistic essence of his father,
Helio's expression of Jiu Jitsu. Helio adapted and innovated
the Japanese style taught to him by Mitsuyo Maeda to fit his
slender frame, and in doing so created a unique approach
to the grappling art transforming it into the simple, yet
sophisticated hybrid system of Gracie Jiu Jitsu, known today
by most people as Brazilian Jiu Jitsu.

"People have developed books with a hundred ways to sweep a person. Why do you sweep, then submit them? Why not just submit them, if your goal is to submit them?"
-Relson Gracie

What is truly amazing is that ALL Brazilian Jiu Jitsu, with literally hundreds of thousands practitioners and hundreds of variations, now practiced all over the world were the result of the research of two brothers Helio and Carlos Gracie, and especially the development and expression of Helio personalizing his Jiu Jitsu so it would be more simple and effective for himself.

"The Jiu-Jitsu that I created was designed to give the weak ones a chance to face the heavy and strong. The primary objective of Jiu-Jitsu is to empower the weak, who for not having the physical attributes are often intimidated. My Jiu-Jitsu is an art of self-defense in which rules and time limits are unacceptable."
-Grand –Master Helio Gracie (October 1, 1913 – January 29, 2009)

Another pioneer of martial arts, Bruce Lee developed a system and philosophy of martial arts based on his personal needs. Bruce began his training in Hong Kong in traditional Gung Fu. His major influence being from a style called Wing Chun. Wing Chun was known for its simplicity, economical movement and use of straight-line attacks. Wing Chun is considered to be one of the most effective systems of Chinese Gun Fu because of its simple, direct approach. But, upon closer examination, in Bruce Lee's mind, Wing Chun was far from what he desired as the ultimate martial art. Lee saw several inadequacies and felt that Wing Chun was good at medium range striking, but lacked ground fighting, evasive footwork, and long range kicking. Bruce saw the need to adapt the simplicity, and as he developed his own personalized approach, he carved away much of what he felt was unessential. According to my teacher Dan Inosanto, Bruce's Jun Fan Gung Fu changed frequently as he evolved it, and in the final days of his life, Bruce Lee had no desire to block, shield or defend passively, he only wanted to attack as his defense. Therefore, his Art and Philosophy of Jeet Kune Do, translated literally as "The Intercepting Fist Way"

"The TRUTH in combat is different for each individual...
1) Research Your Own Experience
2) Absorb What Is Useful
3) Reject What Is Useless
4) Add What Is Specifically Your Own
-Bruce Lee

Bruce Lee sought to create a system of personal martial arts expression that had no limitation, yet was simple and effective. In pursuit of this concept, Bruce Lee established a foundation of personal development, using it to open up the minds of martial artists to cross training, strength and fitness adaptation, equipment training (focus mitt/kicking shield), and the judicious integration of striking and grappling from other styles. Bruce believed that in order to be an exceptional fighter, he must be in exceptional physical condition, and that many of the training methods of other athletes, especially boxers would develop the attributes or qualities in him necessary to be at an extraordinary level. Bruce Lee was a pioneer of American Martial Arts and one of the strongest influences, along with Helio Gracie in the development of **Modern MMA.** There is an intriguing correlation between these two innovative individuals aside from their search for simplicity and effectiveness. Both men learned a martial art, and then adapted it to fit their slender build, developing both themselves and their personal martial art method to an extraordinary level. In addition both used radically different training methods, and by doing these things changed the way most martial artists train, fight and think forever.

"In JKD, one does not accumulate but eliminate. It is not daily increase but daily decrease. The height of cultivation always runs to simplicity. To me, the extraordinary aspect of martial arts lies in its simplicity. The easy way is also the right way, and Martial Arts is nothing at all special; the closer to the true way of Martial Arts, the less wastage of expression there is. In building a statue, a sculptor doesn't keep adding clay to his subject. Actually, he keeps chiseling away at the inessentials until the truth of its creation is revealed without obstructions. Thus, contrary to other styles, being wise in Jeet Kune-Do doesn't mean adding more; it means to minimize, in other words to hack away the unessential. It is not daily increase but daily decrease; hack away the unessential." -Bruce Lee

As a coach and career martial artist, I've observed and trained under some of the best out there. In the sport of **Martial Athletics**, the BEST have a common thread. They are **really good** at a few things and they have a very strong mindset! Kickboxer "Superfoot" Bill Wallace used only three kicks and did them with only his lead foot, yet beat the best at that time period time after time. Muay Thai Champion Rob Kaman has a few favorite combinations and exceptional timing and execution, as does Ramon Deckker. MMA Russian Champion Fedor Emelianenko has three favorite submissions. Judo

Olympian Mike Swain had only a handful of throws. Rickson Gracie's finish is usually a choke. Ajarn Chai Sirisute WILL land his blistering round kick on you. Everyone knows what these individuals will probably do when they fight them, yet these champions rarely lose, if ever, and in most cases, there is nothing you can do to stop them.

As I have observed this, the philosophy known as **Occam's Razor** immediately comes to my mind. There are two parts that are considered the foundation of Occam's Razor, and they were originally written in Latin:

The Principle of Plurality – Plurality should not be posited without necessity.

The Principle of Parsimony – It is pointless to do with more what is done with less.

In other words, the simplest explanation is usually the right one. The term *razor* illustrates the principle of shaving away unnecessary assumptions to get to the simplest explanation. In the reference of Martial Athletic Competition, use as little as possible to get the optimum result.

"It is better to really know one technique very well and know 100 ways to get into that technique."-Dan Inosanto

But, simpler does not mean easier, and before you can carve away the things unessential to your personal expression and character, you must FIRST have a strong foundational mass. You cannot eliminate what you do not have.

This philosophy, applies not just to the physical aspects of MMA training and competition, but is consistently true in the mental aspects as well.

"Simplicity is the ultimate sophistication." -Leonardo da Vinci

How Can You Use This?
Here are eight simple applications to keep in mind.

1) Never start from a conclusion. Study all aspects in their entirety before drawing your final conclusion or answer. Although it may appear that the first and most simple answer must be the right answer, use the science of logic and analysis to help determine the answer. It may just be that the simplest answer, is the correct answer. Be ready to adjust as the situation changes.

2) Remember that there is a constant illusion of control in every moment during competition. The reality is you do not have control of your opponent, you have control over only THREE things: The things you say to yourself (your inner voice), the pictures you make in your head (your visualization), and your actions.

3) E+R=O Your experiences plus your reactions equal your results. You can't control circumstances that occur, but you can control your reaction to what happens, and it is that reaction that will determine your outcome. A simple example of this is, if someone attacks you, you cannot control his actions, but you can control your *re-action*, and your reaction will determine your outcome of his attack.

4) You are only capable of holding ONE thought at a time. You are either winning or losing, you're defeated or you are working it, you either suck or you don't. You're happy at any given moment or you are not. You hate your life or you don't. You can't believe both at the same time. Those thoughts, inner voices and pictures are your choice. If you choose one, the other will **not exist** at that moment in your mind.

5) You pay now or you pay later. But, either way, you PAY.
If you don't train hard now, you pay later when you fight. If you don't do what you need to do to be successful, you pay later with regret, poverty or unhappiness. Either way, you will pay. Have the discipline it takes to pay now. (My son, Erik "Chainsaw" Charles pointed out this concept to me in others.)

6) You become what you think about MOST of the time.
I have a favorite saying, "Your mind always moves in the direction of your dominant thoughts." The result of this profound principle is "You get what you focus on." When you focus on your problems, your mind will be problem focused, in contrast, if you focus on solutions to your problems, your mind will be solution oriented." If you focus on being the *BEST you can be*, you will succeed. This may or may not mean you will be the best, but it will guarantee you will be the best YOU can be.

7) Be simple and direct. Work to be amazingly proficient at a few very important aspects of your GAME, and seek to apply these qualities with exceptional timing.

8) Simplify into threes. Learn, then develop at least three escapes and three attacks that you feel you are best at from each position both standing and on the ground. Three strong options allow you the opportunity to have more than enough tools. This concept was taught to me by one of my coaches and friend, Erik Paulson, founder of CSW. Remember, it's not your knowledge; it is your action that will lead you to success.

"Try to learn at least THREE attacks, Three Escapes and THREE counters from each position, then develop your best three attacks, escapes and counters in each position from there." -Erik Paulson 1991

As you train, remember the important aspect of SIMPLICTY. This is no easy matter, because our human thought is deep and complex. But, learn this fundamental concept well and you will be in the company of some of the most exceptional people in Martial Arts history, both ancient and modern. **Seek simply to simplify!**

"Make everything as simple as possible, but not simpler." -Albert Einstein

"To me, the extraordinary aspect of martial arts lies in Its simplicity. The easy way is also the right way, and martial arts is nothing at all special; the closer to the true way of martial arts, the less wastage of expression there is."
-Bruce Lee

Lesson Twelve
Understanding Your Personal OS

"My body goes to work and I don't have to think or concentrate; actually if I were to think, it would stop the FLOW. It is the flow that is the real power, this is the true genius, it is doing without thought that allows you to tap into your best personal performance."-Kevin Seaman

These days nearly everyone has a computer or at least uses a computer. The system behind the operation of the computer I'm typing on right at this very moment is called the Operating System or OS. You probably understand how to use different programs on your computer, but do you know how your computer's operating system works?

Your brain, although in many ways is like a super mega-computer also has an operating system. We refer to this as "the sub-conscious." Yes, that three pounds of gray tissue between your ears is the most amazing and sophisticated blob of equipment known to man. It controls everything. What you say, what you see, what you feel, and what you do. It also controls how you will PERFORM! If you are a martial artist, a fighter, a competitor or you just want to perform better... read on.

In school, we learn and focus primarily on the conscious mind, we use it to learn, make critical decisions and analyze problems, and in many other ways. It is in the forefront of our awareness and a somewhat tangible. It is our "THINKING MIND", yet it makes up a relatively minor percentage of our brain function. Our sub-conscious, is rarely discussed,
110

hardly understood and makes up for 5/6 of our brain function. However, most people have very little understanding of how to influence and use it, let alone how their sub-conscious mind affects and influences them on a moment-to-moment basis.

The Work Horse

Yes, our conscious mind does choose for us, but our sub-conscious mind transforms these choices into our realities. Why is it important to understand more about your sub-conscious? Your sub-conscious controls 96% of your behavior, what you will or will not accomplish, your habits and a huge list of other important functions in your life. It is your sub-conscious that moves you from point A to point B; it is your conscious mind that tells you to do that. As a Martial Artist or Martial Athlete your sub-conscious is crucial in your success. You may be asking, "If it's so important, why don't we focus more on the understanding of just how to use our OS? " Let's start now!

The Six Intellectual Functions

According to performance expert Bob Proctor, there are six intellectual functions of conscious mind and three sub-conscious functions that help you with other critical issues. As we go through these I will illustrate the basic connections between these functions and how to use them for your personal success.

1) Reason

Your power to reason is the great problem solver. It tells you what possible outcomes you should consider when given a challenge or question. It engages the reticular cortex of your brain in its function as the Reticular Activating System or

RAS. The RAS is like a filter that sorts all the information your brain receives and tells you what is important to you. It points your focus to what you need to survive and what you want (or what you don't want).

2) Perception

Your second intellectual function is perception. According to the dictionary, perception is the process of using the five senses to acquire information about the surrounding environment or situation and then interpreting that information. Your perception is dictated by your beliefs and your values; which are basically beliefs you attach emotion to and therefore value. You don't see with your eyes, you see with your brain. You see the world not how it really is, but by more **as YOU really are**. Your beliefs act as filters that change the way you see the TRUTH and possibilities. You don't really experience reality; you experience your representation of reality. Thus, your beliefs become your reality.

"If you believe, then you have already taken the first step towards your achievement." -Rickson Gracie

3) Will

Man's will is one of the most powerful forces in our world. Your will can enable you to do things you would never dream possible. The force behind will is passion. The more driven you are, the more will you possess to accomplish whatever you seek out to do. Without a strong will, you will never succeed. Your will is a powerful form of psychological leverage driven by your mental toughness, it keeps you pushing ahead regardless of the opposing challenge. Your will is demonstrated through persistence. Once your will has been broken, you have given up. Will is like a muscle, the more you use it, the stronger it becomes.

4) Memory

Your memory is like a record of everything you see, feel, hear, smell, taste and do. It records these experiences and bits of information and attaches emotion (either positive or negative) to them known as associations. These associations are so powerful, that it is like a having a preconceived recorded impression of what you feel about everything that's happened to you, and a record of everything you've ever experienced with your five senses. Sometimes, these memories become buried in your sub-conscious, because they are so painful or contradictory to what you believe, but they will still control your behavior, you just don't know why.

5) Imagination

Your imagination explores the world of possibility by using visual pictures, or mental imagery. The amazing thing about mental imagery is the more detail and realism that you can place in those visualizations, the closer it becomes to an experienced reality. Although your imagination is manifested by your conscious thought, your sub-conscious cannot determine whether these vivid imagined experiences are real experiences. Studies have been shown that almost the exact brain function occurs when you visualize with extreme detail, as if it were really happening. Everything man has created is at first created in the mind, before it takes physical form.

"I am enough of an artist to draw freely upon my imagination. Imagination is more important than knowledge. Knowledge is limited.

Imagination encircles the world." - Albert Einstein

6) Intuition

Intuition is a function of knowing or believing something instinctively without actual evidence for it. It's like, a "vibe" or feeling that something is right or not. It also helps you detect the presence of danger. It's a "gut" feeling really. Some believe it's an awareness of a vibration of the cells on a molecular level. Intuition is also linked to your perception, so pay attention.

Where'd It Go?

According to John Assaraf in his book Having It All, at any given time, your conscious mind is absorbing about 11 million pieces of information, you're only aware of between 40 and 2,000 pieces. So, what happened to the other 10 million something pieces? You dropped them from your consciousness because you either conditioned your brain to drop them or you didn't need them. John goes on to say, that the part of your brain that processes conscious awareness, conscious thought and conscious behavior, as well as, willpower and persistence only encompasses about 17% of your brain's mass. Now this is important...so, pay attention! Your conscious mind only controls between two and four percent of your perceptions and your behavior! Your "Personal OS", your Personal Operating System controls MOST of your behavior. Your sub-conscious mind is the reason your brain has an unlimited potential.

The Three Functions Of The Sub-conscious

1) Operates All Your Bodily Functions

Your sub-conscious is what keeps you conscious. It is

114

responsible for all your body's functions on an autonomic level. Feel your heart beat, breathe in…that's your sub-conscious at work.

2) Warehouse For All Your Memories, Habits and Beliefs

Your sub-conscious runs the OS program for your learning system. Through repetition, you have developed your habits, which are deeply ingrained in your sub-conscious. From there, your sub-conscious runs the habit pattern each time it perceives necessary, regardless of it's benefit or detriment to you. It's now part of your conditioned behavior, just like your associations and your beliefs; these now control your behavioral responses, most times without you realizing it.

3) Your Sub-conscious Energy

This is the area of your sub-conscious that connects you in a sense with energy on a non-physical level. Everything in the nature is made up of energy, millions of different frequencies of energy. Energy is in a constant and continual state of motion.

"The intelligent energy in you is connected to all other energy fields and intelligence, and whatever you want in your life begins with desire and thought." -John Assaraf

Like attracts like, negative emotions attract negative, positive thoughts attract positive. Most people focus on exactly what they DON'T want and attract just exactly that. In life, you get what you focus on. If you go into the cage with the focus that you don't want to get hurt, you WILL leave the cage hurt. If you look at your fight as an opportunity for experience and focus on performing at your best, that is what your energy will bring you!

How Can I Use This?

Work to learn and understand as much as you can about your brain and how to manage your sub-conscious mind. Your Personal OS is the key to excelling at your potential in the Martial Arts. Here are a few tips to get you started on your Mind Game.

1) **Reason** Use both your insight and the insight of a mentor, coach or skilled professional to help develop your ability to reason. In MMA, as in other competitive arenas, it's not always the better athlete or technician that wins. Many times it's the right strategy that determines success.

2) Perception

Become extremely tuned into your perception. Learn about how you can strengthen your empowering beliefs and change your disempowering beliefs. Try to perceive what you see, feel and believe from more than one frame of reference. I cover beliefs in great detail in my book, The Winning Mind Set.

3) Will

Develop your will and you will be a force to be reckoned with. Will is about passion. Remember, the "why" we do something is always more powerful than any "what" or "how". Attack your training and your development with passion and persistence. Develop a stronger "Will" by bombarding you're your sub-conscious with personal self-made audio recordings, verbal affirmations and written notes of "**what** you want, **why** you want it and **how** you will get it." This absolute sub-conscious saturation of positive reinforcement will strengthen your WILL to an unstoppable level.

4) Memory

Work to strengthen your positive associations and diminish your negative associations where needed. Use anchors in conjunction with visualization to tap into your sub-conscious. Many times athletes will create stress by focusing on past losses, and then repeat their poor performance because it was imbedded in their sub-conscious. Learn more about the how to use the power of your associations to past experiences, I touch on these in great detail in my book, The Winning Mind Set and past Authority MMA Magazine articles.

5) Imagination

Practice, not just in the gym, but in your *Mind Gym* as well. By visualizing over and over in your head exactly and precisely what you want to accomplish in the fight, with your technique and in your performance, you will become 10X the athlete you were capable of through mere physical training. If you cut kick your trainer 20X in training and 50X in your head, you've just not only improved your cut kick technically, but you've improved your success ratio. Because guess what? You will always do it better and more consistent in your visualizations than you do when you perform physically. Repetition is the mother of skill, and as my friend World Class trainer Greg Nelson says, "Practice makes HABIT." If you practice it right, it's habit, if you practice it wrong it's still habit.

6) Intuition

Use your intuition to read your opponent's intention. If you pay close attention, you can tell what his level of confidence is and in what area he may be weaker or more powerful than you. This intuitive information can give you insight into how to strategize your approach.

Remember, your sub-conscious is the KEY to your behavior, performance and ultimate success. Although your conscious mind may be very strong, when paired with the power of your sub-conscious, you will be optimal in your performance! According to Professor Relson Gracie, his father Helio believed that success in Jiu Jitsu was 90% mental and 10% physical. Hmm...something to carefully consider, wouldn't you say?

"I figured that if I said it enough, I would convince the world that I really was the greatest." -Muhammad Ali

7 Keys To Making The Most Out Of Your Training Experience

As you enter your training in MMA and begin your progression within the Martial Arts here are 7 Key principles that will help you to accelerate your training, learn faster and retain what you're taught more effectively, making your experience the most optimal.

1) When you arrive at your MMA gym clear your mind of all thoughts not associated with your goal of learning. The distractions, challenges, stress and work of everyday life will still be there after your class has ended. Be there 100%, absorbing the material with all of your attention.

2) In order to learn anything well and become excellent at it, you need to approach it seriously. There is an abundance of material presented in each session. Buy a notebook designated for your Martial Arts Studies and take notes after each class. It is impossible to absorb the details and remember them without notes.

3) Ask mindful questions of yourself after class as you reflect on a technique or concept taught to you and ask the instructor during your next class to clarify any points you didn't understand, or questions relating to how you might use what you've learned effectively.

4) Develop your visualization skills. Once you've learned a technique, see yourself performing the technique

correctly over and over in your Mind's Eye. This mental strategy is used by some of the top athletes and best fighters in the world to assist them in their success.

5) Create a Goal Sheet of exactly what you want to accomplish in your program. Make approximate time deadlines and for your goals and sub-goals. Sub-goals help you to see progress in a step-by-step process, while deadlines keep you on track to accomplishing your goals.

6) I can tell you that consistency is one of the most important aspects to developing any skill and meeting the objectives you wish to accomplish. I know this because I have achieved the ranks of 8 Black Belts and recently started on my journey to my 9th as a white belt. The secret of how I accomplished this is through consistency.

7) Develop an attitude of championship standards. Always approach learning something new, with an open mind. Trust your teachers, and respect what they offer. Take care of your training partner and use each other to become the BEST you both can be. As my Thai Boxing instructor, Master Chai Sirisute has said; Be hard like a diamond and smooth like silk.

<u>20 Key Principles To Remember</u>

1) Our mind always leads us in the direction of our dominant thoughts.

2) Your BELIEFS, become your REALITY.

3) Going with what comes. This quality is the ability to make the very best out of every experience and outcome.

4) In every career endeavor there is a set of 5-6 specific skill sets known as Critical Success Factors, that are crucial to the high level success of that challenge. The more exceptional your personal CSF's, the greater your success will be in your GAME!

5) When using the Associative Anchor strategy for success visualize with vividness, frequency, consistency, and duration, and you will see amazing results in your overall performance.

6) Reframing is a method of changing the way we may look at something, changing the meaning and there by changing the emotion attached to the previous view or frame of reference.

7) You get what you FOCUS on!

8) Your mind can only focus on one thought at a time.
122

It can switch back and forth, but ultimately you can't think two things simultaneously.

9) Always focus on what you want, never on what you don't want.

10) People who succeed are those who...
• Know <u>specifically</u> what they want!
• Have developed the ability to take consistent <u>action</u>.
• Have persistence. They <u>don't give up!</u>
• Learn from their end results.

11) Remember there is no such thing as unreasonable goals, just unreasonable time frames.

12) If you don't like the answer, ask a BETTER question. Questions are extremely powerful tools for changing our mindsets. Asking questions can do three things. It can change what we focus on, it can change what we delete, and it can give us access to different resources (who, what, where, how, when) to help achieve our desired ends.

13) Elevate Your Standards! You cannot play or think at the level you were at as an amateur fighting as a Professional. What got you here will not get you where you want to be.

14) Seek to Simplify. Focus on the foundational basics, develop a nearly flawless execution of simplicity.

15) Never start from a conclusion. Study all aspects in their entirety before drawing your final conclusion or answer.

16) E+R=O: Your experiences plus your reactions equal your results. You can't control circumstances that occur, but you can control your reaction to what happens, and it is that reaction that will determine your outcome.

17) You pay now or you pay later. But, either way, you PAY. If you don't train hard now, you pay later when you fight.

18) Like attracts like, negative emotions attract negative, positive thoughts attract positive. Most people focus on exactly what they DON'T want and attract just exactly that.

19) Practice, not just in the gym, but in your *Mind Gym* as well. Visualize over and over in your head exactly and precisely what you want to accomplish in the fight.

20) Repetition is the Mother Of Skill. Repeat the fundamentals in this book over and over, until you can recite them when asked and recall them when needed. That's HOW you get really great at anything! Now, Are You Ready? In the words of Big John McCarthy, "Let's Get It On!"

Journal Entries

Journal Entries

Journal Entries

Journal Entries

Journal Entries

Asked what surprises the Dalai Lama most, "Man. Because he sacrifices his health in order to make money. Then he sacrifices his money to recuperate his health. And then he is so anxious about the future that he does not enjoy the present; the result being that he does not live in the present or the future; he lives as if he is never going to die, and then he dies never having really lived."

Check Out Kevin Seaman and Jim Brault's Book

The Winning Mind Set
Unleash The Power Of Your Mind
Here are some reader reviews

"Simply Brilliant!"
Jon "Bones" Jones
UFC Light Heavyweight Champion

"The Winning Mind Set is a fantastic weapon that gives you the firepower to really succeed"
-Kenny Florian
UFC Fighter

"Your attitude determines your altitude even more than your aptitude. This book shows you how to win from within in every area."
-Brian Tracy
Author of over 40 books, Consultant for many Fortune 500 Companies

"The Winning Mind Set has helped me to restructure my thinking for more effective training and success as a Professional Athlete. I would recommend The Winning Mind Set to anyone looking to develop a winning mindset of their own."
- Tamdan "The Barn Cat" McCrory
Professional MMA Fighter
UFC Veteran

KEVIN SEAMAN'S VIDEO DVDs

Jun Fan Gung Fu – Concepts and Principles of Jeet Kune Do –
Vol 1/2 Seeking the Path

Jun Fan Gung Fu – Concepts and Principles of Jeet Kune Do –
Vol 3/4 Basic Tool Development

Filipino Martial Arts Vol 1

BOOKS

Jun Fan Gung Fu
Seeking The Path Of Jeet Kune Do
Paperback/Digital

The Winning Mind Set
Unleash The Power Of Your Mind
Kevin Seaman/Jim Brault
Paperback/Audiobook/Digital

The Mind Game Of MMA
12 Lessons To Develop The Mental Toughness
Essential To Becoming A Champion
Kevin Seaman
Paperback/ Digital/ Audiobook to be Released Winter 2012

Both the above videos and books are available from:
Kevin Seaman c/o East West Martial Arts, LLC
326 Barrington Rd.
Syracuse, NY 13214
Phone: (607) 423-5159
www.ewmaa.com
www.thewinningmindset.com